THE
INFLATABLE
KAYAK
HANDBOOK

THE
INFLATABLE
KAYAK
HANDBOOK

Melinda Allan

Johnson Books • Boulder, Colorado

Cover design by Molly Gough

Library of Congress Cataloging-in-Publication Data
Allan, Melinda.
   The inflatable kayak handbook / Melinda Allan. — 1st ed.
   p.   cm.
   Includes bibliographic references (p.   ).
   ISBN 1-55566-078-9 (pbk.)
   1. Kayaking. 2. Kayaks. I. Title.
GV783.A45   1991
797.1'22—dc20   91-11036
                                                         CIP

Printed in the United States of America by
Johnson Publishing Company
1880 South 57th Court
Boulder, Colorado 80301

⊕ Printed on recycled paper with soy ink

To my mother, Mary Frances Craft Allan,
without whom I would not have been possible.

CONTENTS

ACKNOWLEDGMENTS

Writing a book is a long, difficult, and demanding task, made easier by friends who share their specialized information. Thanks to Susan Baxter and Mel Jackson for their encouragement when I needed it the most. Lee, with the Boat People, and Dan, with B & A Distributors, and the folks at AIRE provided much-needed information cheerfully.

A special thanks to kayaker David Gilmore, who camped in a reversal so I could get photographs. Thanks also to Fred Faust and his son Owen for their patience with a picky photographer, and to Jeff Bennett and Mike Doyle, both with Beyond Limits, who proved that IKs really can run Class V whitewater.

Finally, I must express my appreciation to Al Law, of Wild Water Adventures, without whom I would still be struggling with heavy backpacks, blistered feet, and no Cokes to drink.

INTRODUCTION
The Inflatable Kayak Revolution

Time to play human pinball again! Quick backward strokes of the double-bladed paddle stall your inflatable kayak, allowing a few more seconds to appraise the situation. Like most steep rapids, "Bull's-eye" remains invisible to boaters seated at water level until the very last moment. Staring down into a maze of boulders and spray, you suddenly realize that no clear route exists. Then the current grabs hold of your little boat.

Windmilling the paddle sends the inflatable kayak (IK) flying into the only open water, a slim slot on the far left side, barely clearing a pair of boulders. True to the rapid's name, the current slams hard into another boulder smack in the middle of the river. A quick turn avoids this hazard, but dumps your IK sideways over a kitchen sink-sized rock. You lean hard downstream, bracing with the paddle, and escape with only your boat swamped and your dignity dampened. The IK is waterlogged for only a moment before the self-bailing boat drains water out through four holes carved in the fabric floor. Maneuverable again, you arrive at the bottom of your first technical Class IV rapid upright . . . although unceremoniously backwards.

A merry ride, typical of the rapids you and your companions will encounter while running this remote desert river at extremely low water levels. You laugh and shout in victory, your exuberance tempered by a firm decision to scout the next major drop from shore, where the view is better. Although you have rammed rocks, wiggled through passages almost too tight to accommodate the yard-wide boats, and dragged the IKs over gravel bars, the tough, bullet-shaped inflatable kayaks remain undamaged.

Paddling isn't usually this tiring, but today you've pushed extra miles. In your excitement, you haven't realized how tired you are from the day's battle with Class IV drops and upriver winds until you reach camp, a small beach below a noisy riffle. Darkness comes rapidly in a deep river canyon; your companions scurry around, finishing chores quickly. Soon, tense shoulder muscles are soothed by one of nature's most marvelous creations, the wilderness hot spring, as you ease into the delightful 103-degree water. As you soak, the night deepens. You listen to the music of the river. Above you flows a river of stars, rimmed by black canyon walls. Somewhere an owl begins hooting.

This river is a special place, one that attracts several thousand other boaters every spring. But for the next week, you won't see another person—other than your paddling companions—as you guide your inflatable kayak downstream. On this trip, the big cave will be untrammeled, the next hot springs camp also empty, and the fish still hungry. Drought throughout the West has altered the float plans of many parties; abysmally low water levels bar use of traditional river craft. But you have faith in the tough little cocoon of fabric and air insulating your body . . . you must, for the nearest road is forty miles away, beyond the straight-up, 400-foot rock walls. Many rapids will be like Bull's-eye—tight and rocky, barely wide enough for the inflatable kayaks to wiggle through, and in a few places you'll be forced to carry for safety. There will be a million razor-edged rocks, impossible to dodge, so you'll crash into them— and keep on going. A few years ago, such a journey would have been impossible.

Rafts attempting to float this scenic stretch would have been stranded in shallows around the first bend of the river. Older IK models made of thin, cheap materials would have been torn to shreds. Canoes and hardshell kayaks would take a beating, would never carry you through the tight passages with the hundred pounds of food and gear you have stowed behind your seat, and these craft might prove dangerous if tipped over in the low water. In some of the steep, shallow drops, the pointed bow of a hardshell kayak might dive beneath a rock and "pin" or trap the unfortunate paddler, something that would never happen in the open cockpit of the inflatable kayak. And your ten-foot-long IKs can thread through the narrow slots much more easily than a seventeen-foot canoe or twelve-foot kayak. Only the modern inflatable kayak is suitable for your expedition.

The world of whitewater boating is enjoying a quiet revolution. Space Age technology has finally caught up with the Stone Age urge to explore new places. First came new developments in raft fabrics and design, which had gone mostly unchanged since World War II surplus rafts started showing up on rivers. More recently, those improvements have been used on the inflatable kayak. As with most revolutions in technology, it has taken awhile for people to adjust and adapt, to learn about and take advantage of new possibilities.

At first glance, these little boats appear fragile and tippy. Many people are a little wary of the inflatable kayak, until they climb into one and start paddling. Then there's that intimidating "kayak" label, which links the IK with those hardshell kayakers who've earned a reputation for kamikaze stunts. Unfortunately, this daredevil image includes all kayak-like craft, and continues to plague the inflatable version. But IKs don't deserve this bad rap; they are far more stable, safer, and easier for beginners to paddle than hardshell models. Poor performance by early, cheap IK versions has also contributed to prejudice against these boats, but the newer, stronger models offer much-improved performance.

A typical inflatable kayak. The paddler sits in an open cockpit, unencumbered by spray skirt or deck. The large side tubes provide flotation and stability and accommodate lots of gear besides. This IK has four separate air chambers: two tubes, thwart, and inflatable floor.

HOW IKS DIFFER FROM OTHER BOATS

The inflatable kayak is, perhaps, more properly called an inflatable canoe—especially if you ask a "hardshell" purist. But its similarity to regular kayaks has made the name inflatable kayak, often shortened to IK, the one in popular use. The IK is a small inflatable boat, usually about thirty-six inches wide and from eight to twelve feet in length. They are made, not of rubber, but of a variety of fabrics, usually forms of PVC or nylon, coated with synthetic forms of rubber for durability. Early versions of the IK looked like bananas: bright yellow, curved to a point at both ends. This is the Tahiti, developed back in 1965 by Sevylor, the boat that made inflatable kayaking famous. Despite its limitations, this boat has been paddled across the world in all kinds of water—lakes, rivers, and oceans. Tahitis have even been paddled down the Colorado River through the Grand Canyon. The Tahiti's great advantage over other models is price: you can still buy a Tahiti at a discount store for under $150.

An IK has two side tubes that, when inflated, form the hull of the boat. Both tubes narrow to a point at the bow and stern, with these tips joined and reinforced for added strength in the better

A hardshell kayak and paddler. The hardshell differs from an inflatable in that the cockpit (space where the paddler sits) is decked over to keep out water. The sides are lower and the boat is narrow, so the hardshell is very maneuverable, but not very stable, especially in the hands of a beginner.

brands. Some sort of seat is usually added, crossways to the tubes, providing back support for the paddler, and—more importantly—serving as a stiffener to keep the tubes from folding inward.

Unlike the traditional hardshell kayaks, most IKs are not decked over, or covered across the top to keep out spray. In addition, the IK features an open cockpit, allowing the paddler to enter and exit the boat easily. A hardshell kayak is actually "worn" by the paddler, sort of like a sit-in garment that floats you. With an IK, you just sit in the open space between the two air-filled tubes, generally on a cushion. A hardshell kayak is designed to hold the paddler inside the boat, even when the boat goes upside-down. That's why the maneuver to get the hardshell kayak back upright—known as the Eskimo roll—must be learned early. If you tip over in a hardshell kayak and do nothing, you can be in real trouble. Traditional kayaks are difficult to get back into after you've taken an unexpected swim—and must also be bailed out before you can resume paddling—so mastering that roll is essential. No such special skills are necessary, however, when paddling an inflatable kayak; if you spill, you just climb back in and try again.

Both hardshell and inflatable kayaks are usually powered by a double-bladed kayak paddle, especially when paddled solo. Canoeists, on the other hand, use single-blade, T-grip paddles. In a canoe, when balance is important—especially when running whitewater—paddlers must kneel in their boats. Kayakers of all breeds sit down with legs forward to maintain balance.

Air is the important difference between the IK and hardshells such as canoes, kayaks, dories, and driftboats. Because they are made of rigid materials, such as plastic, wood, or fiberglass, hardshells possess certain handling characteristics. Rigid boats generate less friction against the water's surface, and therefore handle better than most inflatables. Smaller boats also generate less friction on the water's surface than larger craft. So, a small, rigid boat will maneuver better than a large, floppy one. Of all whitewater craft, hardshell kayaks move and turn the quickest. They are also quite tippy, unforgiving for beginners, and take time to master. Modern IK designs compare favorably with kayaks, and actually handle low water better.

Rafts, of course, are large water craft. They can carry groups of people, but are cumbersome when compared to IKs. They are handy for carrying gear, but do not offer the adventure and excitement of a small, light boat with a single paddler going one-on-one against the river. Due to their oval design, even small rafts will not handle as well as long, narrow craft like IKs.

ADVANTAGES OF THE INFLATABLE KAYAK

Inflatable kayaks were designed as a small play boat for use on flat water like lakes, but soon began to turn up everywhere else, from whitewater rivers to small streams, and even on ocean swells. IKs are versatile. You don't have to run them down rivers, although they operate most efficiently on water with some current. They're great play boats on ponds, lakes, or sloughs. You can fish from them, surf the waves and play games with the river in them, paddle them into the wilderness on a week-long campout, or just mess around in them with your kids. Paddling, in flat water or fast water, offers a good aerobic workout and builds and tones the upper body muscles.

A small boat, usually paddled by one person, the IK puts you close to the water, offering a dramatic sense of scale. Those choppy rapids that looked like nothing from shore loom ahead of you like Niagara Falls when paddling into them in your IK. In need of excitement? You don't have to go looking for world-class whitewater with an IK—whatever's in your own backyard will usually start that adrenalin flowing, when glimpsed from the cockpit of your IK, low over the water's surface. And with the IK's flotation, you'll get a good ride over the waves.

A hardshell kayaker in full gear tests the stability of an inflatable kayak by standing in it.

Women are flocking to IK paddling because they can easily handle the boats by themselves—both on and off the water.

True, as small boats, IKs are more prone to overturning in heavy water, but unlike big rafts, IKs are able to dart across the river's surface like water striders, avoiding the worst spots. Good IK paddlers with solid equipment now regularly run serious whitewater that used to be off-limits for small inflatables.

A major reason for the IK's soaring popularity is instant fun. The basic skills are easy to learn, and most people pick them up very quickly. Instead of spending weeks in classes and swimming pools, you're out there on the river. Of course, learning how to run a river in any type of craft takes some time, but the IK speeds your progress. There are only two basic strokes to learn, and no difficult Eskimo roll to master. Getting in and out is a cinch, and so is balancing. Standard IK design favors the novice paddler. IKs are more "forgiving" of beginners' mistakes—a missed stroke need not result in an upset. For novices, IKs smooth out tricky currents and swirling eddy waters without need of fancy strokes. They are very maneuverable: only the hardshell kayak has a shorter turning radius than the IK, which means the IK fits between rocks easier and with less effort than most all other whitewater craft.

The one-on-one IK experience—you and the river—provides excitement and challenge. You are in charge of your own destiny. You decide where to go, how to run a rapid, and how fast and how far you want to progress with your boating skills. No one but you can dictate whether to keep pushing your limits, or to settle back in comfortable, moderate waters. If you want a relaxing trip, or an adrenalin-charged adventure, the choice is yours.

Low water is seldom a problem for the IK. Many American paddlers obtained their first IKs during the droughts in western states in recent years. IKs were the only whitewater boats that could navigate the reduced flows of most rivers with ease, and still offer an exciting ride. IKs were made to tackle low water. The new IKs are so light and strong, you can almost paddle them on a heavy dew.

IKs offer a wonderful way for families to enjoy time together. A father paddles his son through a Class III rapid on the McKenzie River in Oregon, skillfully aiming for a safe route around the turbulence in the foreground. The one-person inflatable kayak readily accommodates an adult and a small child, or children can paddle alone on more moderate water.

Should you ground out on a midstream "sleeper" rock, you can wiggle your rump to get yourself free; if you're stuck on a shoal, simply get out and push. These boats bounce off what rocks you can't paddle around. Once you have mastered the necessary skills, possibilities for IK trips are unlimited.

Across the country, there are thousands of streams too small or with too many portages to interest other boaters, just waiting to be explored by inflatable kayak. From such an abundance, the paddler can readily choose the level of involvement desired, whether raging whitewater through a lonely desert gorge, or a quiet paddle through the suburbs. Day trips offer a rewarding way to spend a Saturday getting away from it all, without spending the time and planning necessary for a longer trip. In many areas of the country, a memorable IK drift can be launched underneath a city bridge, just minutes from your home.

As inflatables, IKs are lightweight and easy to handle alone, even by small people. They weigh between 15 and 40 pounds, a manageable portage burden. There is no pressure to run water beyond your ability when your boat is easy to carry around a rapid. In rugged country, you can deflate the IK and roll it up, carry it around an obstacle, then pump it back up in five minutes and be back on the water. And, compared to other whitewater craft, inflatable kayaks are easy to rig: no cramming flotation bags below the deck, no stomping on foot pumps for an hour.

Transportation to water's edge was never easier: everything fits into the tiniest compact car, and the airlines won't balk at the sight of them. You can even utilize public transportation to launch your IK adventure. They're convenient—set-up time is short, putting you on the water well ahead of the larger, slower rafts. Of course, if you're in a hurry, sturdy IKs can be carried by cartop to the water's edge, without a roof rack. The IK's compactability adds to its versatility. You can paddle exotic locations like Hawaii or Alaska without shipping problems, and if you want to really get away from it all, pack your IK onto a bush plane, the back of a horse, or even on a llama.

And the IK's virtues don't stop at river's end. Part of their increasing popularity is due to their compactness. For apartment dwellers, IKs are the perfect boat. Even the largest two-man IK will, when deflated, roll into a package small enough to stow under the bed or on a shelf in the hall closet. Paddles come in break-down styles, eliminating another storage hassle.

One vital feature of the modern IK is its inherent safety. The new IK designs are more stable than ever; in most models, you can even stand up. If they should tip over, uprighting them is quick and easy. The best models feature self-bailing floors, so you won't sit for long in cold water or worry about the boat being swamped beyond control after hitting a big wave. The IK has built-in flotation, which means there's no need to add special air bags to keep it afloat in case of upset. Also standard in quality models are multiple air chambers, so even if a tube is damaged, the IK will still float. Rigid foam floors are often added to improve handling and self-bailing characteristics—these also add a measure of safety, since they are incapable of deflating.

With its open cockpit design, an IK can't trap a boater inside, as sometimes occurs in hardshell kayaks, which have been known to collapse on their owners. (Even if the IK did manage to pin you against a rock, you could cut yourself free quickly with a good river knife. Cutting through the polyethelene plastic of a hardshell kayak with a knife is next to impossible.) Because it's light, small, and filled with air, the IK almost never endangers a capsized paddler. A hardshell boat can become a deadly missile when you're floating beside it instead of sitting in it, and even rafts have been known to injure ejected boaters by squeezing them against boulders. Instead of becoming a danger to the swimmer, an IK offers protection and flotation.

Sitting in an IK is quite comfortable. You are surrounded by inflated cushions, supported by a firm backrest. If the boat you select isn't totally comfortable, custom seating can be added to make those long paddling days more pleasant. Your feet aren't cramped up inside a small cockpit, as they are in a hardshell kayak, and you don't have to kneel on hard surfaces, like canoeists. In fact, the IK offers a fine opportunity for people with minor lower-body problems, bad knees in particular, to enjoy whitewater sport and wilderness exploration.

In an IK, you explore the wilderness sitting down, back braced against a comfortable foam or inflated seat, with cargo piled

In an IK, you explore wilderness sitting down. This paddler is enjoying a quiet stretch of Oregon's famous Rogue River.

behind. IKs designed for two people will easily carry one paddler plus lots of backcountry gear—enough for several weeks at a time. With the assistance of river currents, you paddle, not pack, the load. On many rivers, you paddle only to keep the boat tracking, and to maneuver around obstacles. The river does most of the work.

IKs hold more weight than backpacks, and can carry more in volume than hardshell kayaks, without sacrificing as much maneuverability or making the boat drag bottom. They are ideal for small persons, who may have difficulty carrying heavy loads in their backpacks. There's even room for those little luxuries usually left behind on go-light backpack trips, such as hardcover books, canned food, pillows, or even some steaks packed in one of the newfangled soft coolers. Larger people, sometimes cramped in small boats, will fit the bigger IKs easily—and still have room left over for gear.

Best of all, IKs are silent. Only the splash of the paddle betrays your presence. Wild animals and birds may often be approached more closely than is possible in a clunky canoe.

And, as you found out during your less-than-perfect descent of Bull's-eye Rapid, the new IKs are rugged. Constructed of sturdy, tear-resistant nylon fabrics and special coatings, IKs bounce off rocks with impunity. They last for years, with minimal care. Tougher fabrics and coatings have changed IKs from flimsy toys to serious river craft. It's still hard for some folks to accept the idea that IKs aren't "rubber duckies" any longer. These are not boats that will dissolve underneath you on day two of a week-long paddle—they are boats you can count on.

1

EQUIPMENT
Weaving Through the Inflatable Kayak Jungle

A few years ago, selecting an inflatable kayak was easy. Paddlers were pretty much limited to the Tahiti, a thin vinyl "inflatable canoe" imported from France by Sevylor, and its imitators. It was cheap, easy to obtain, and fun to paddle, until you tried to tackle serious whitewater or carry a load. The fun ended when you tired of putting the river back into the river twenty times an hour, or if you ran over a protruding stick and ruined the entire inflatable vinyl floor beyond repair, or simply stressed the vinyl beyond its limits.

Now that manufacturers of quality whitewater rafts are making IKs that are just as tough and dependable as their rafts, paddling an IK will never be the same. The consumer's role has become more challenging, however, as a bewildering array of IK designs, features, materials, and coatings have cropped up. Dozens of different IK models are distributed across the country, with new manufacturers jumping on the bandwagon and an occasional company abandoning the market altogether. Choosing an IK has become complicated and confusing for beginners, and even veteran river rats without IK experience find themselves a little lost in this jungle.

Deciding on a particular IK model isn't terribly difficult if you can narrow your choices by focusing on how your IK will be used. Before you begin to look at IKs—in stores or catalogs—think about how you will use the boat, and what kinds of water you want to paddle. For example, a wider IK design with large tubes is appropriate for "big" whitewater (high-volume rivers with tall waves), while a narrower, shorter IK is better suited to "technical" whitewater (lower-volume rivers with lots of rocks to dodge). If you will be running rocky rivers, you'll need an IK with a tough skin, otherwise you'll spend lots of time patching. Do you want to play in rapids, surfing your IK on a big wave? Then a small, sporty, high-perform-ance model is what you need. Or are you more interested in using your IK for wilderness expeditions? If so, make sure you get one with enough capacity to carry the load you'll be packing. On milder waters, a basic, inexpensive vinyl IK like the Tahiti may fit your needs. If you're interested in sea kayaking, special models are avail-able, with new designs in the works.

Even the best, most expensive IK on the market today won't incorporate all of the desirable design features. So selecting an IK necessitates some compromise. Occasionally, it's possible to add the extras you find you need after the purchase, and sometimes it's best to obtain a second IK that fills a different need.

It's important to consider how serious you are about paddling. If you're not certain this is your sport, consider renting an IK for a day, trying a friend's boat, or joining an outfitted river trip where there will be IKs to experiment with, and certainly do this before you invest in a top-of-the-line model. If you paddle only moderate waters, and don't go out often, perhaps an inexpensive vinyl IK will satisfy your thirst for adventure, without making a big dent in your wallet. You can always purchase a better model when you outgrow the limitations of a vinyl IK.

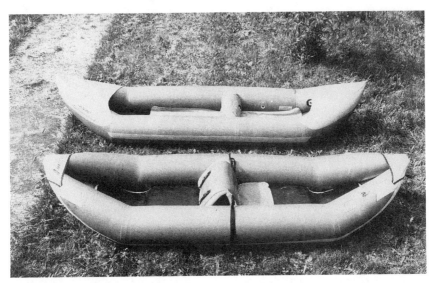

A comparison of two inflatable kayaks. The top IK has an air mattress floor combined with an ethafoam floor. The bottom IK has an all-foam floor. Note the differences in spray shields and seats.

Costs vary dramatically, depending on how an IK is made, what kind of materials are used and the number of features it offers. While vinyl IKs can be easily acquired for around $150 new (down to $50 or less used), quality brands can cost up to $1000 or more. Why such a price range? Cost of labor is a major factor: low-priced vinyl IKs have machine-welded seams (which don't last very long, especially under stress), while costlier models are built by hand. The materials used in IK construction also affect costs: a light vinyl is considerably cheaper than a heavy-duty nylon fabric, and the strong protective coatings used on better boats are another added cost. Remember, however, that a quality IK, treated right, can give you a decade (or more) of paddling pleasure.

One advantage of the constant change in the industry is the availability of bargain-basement close-outs. When a line of IKs is discontinued, the manufacturer often cuts the price in order to get rid of the backlog. An alert paddler can save big bucks, especially if the model is an older IK that is not self-bailing, a feature much in demand these days. If you don't plan to jump into big whitewater right away, you can get by with an IK that is not self-bailing. Or, you can convert the floor to self-bailing yourself, and save the cost difference.

Because the IK manufacturing scene is changing so rapidly, it's difficult to discuss specific brands and models. What is the hottest IK on the market today may be in tomorrow's garage sale. Instead of focusing on a particular name, concentrate on what features you want, and look for an IK that has them.

What kind of features should you look for? The best IKs are built to last. They resist abrasion, punctures, and the ultraviolet rays of the sun. They are easy to paddle downriver and turn on a dime, yet are stable in rapids so you don't get dumped. They are designed to bail water automatically. They have strong seams that hold air inside and dependable valves that operate easily. They can carry both a paddler and gear for an extended adventure. They are comfortable to sit in, and are pleasing to the eye.

SIZE SELECTION

The first consideration is size: how long and how wide should your IK be? Size is important because both length and width determine an IK's capacity—how much of a load the craft can handle safely. Size also influences how the boat handles. Smaller, narrower IKs turn quicker than larger, wider IKs, but the bigger, broader

Tandem paddling in a K-2, the Hyside "Padillac," one of the few K-2s really roomy enough to accommodate two paddlers comfortably. Because most K-2s are smaller, and paddlers need to stroke in coordination, many prefer to paddle them solo.

designs are more stable and are less likely to overturn in big water. Longer boats track (hold a straight-line course without constant paddle correction) better and are superior in windy conditions. Consider also how compact an IK will be when deflated and rolled up, a vital consideration if you want to take your IK on an airplane, stuff it into the trunk of your car, or carry it on a bicycle.

Standard IK models are almost always available in two sizes. The smaller size ranges from about nine to ten feet in length and is sometimes classified as a "1-person" or "K-1" boat by dealers. Longer versions—over ten feet and up to twelve feet—usually are designated "2-person" or "K-2." Special IK designs—particularly sea kayaks—may be even longer. Also appearing on the scene are frisky little IKs shorter than nine feet, designed as exciting "play boats." In other words, they're sports cars, not station wagons. Generally, a K-1 will average about thirty-six inches wide and a K-2 will run up to forty inches across. Measuring is done from the outside of the tubes, so the inside compartment where you sit will be smaller, depending on tube diameter.

Keep in mind your body size requirements when choosing your IK, especially if you are large (over 200 pounds) or petite (under 100 pounds). IKs are sized for the "average" boater, but tend to run

The boat on the left is a K-2 with a single paddler and his gear. On the right is a K-1 for comparison.

small, particularly in the leg compartment. Large or long-legged boaters are more comfortable—and safer—in a two-person IK.

The designation "2-person" is a misnomer, because in most IKs the dual compartments just aren't big enough to accommodate two average people comfortably for any length of time, although they can be a fun tandem boat for day trips or quiet waters. A K-1 is suitable for an adult and a smaller child to paddle together in moderate whitewater. Coordinated paddling between two people using double-bladed kayak paddles takes practice. Generally, two people who want to paddle together in whitewater or on an extended trip are better off using two separate IKs, usually K-1s, instead of a single large boat. However, a K-2 does make a great wilderness expedition boat, even for an average-sized person, because of the space available for carrying extra gear.

On the other hand, a smaller person may not have the strength to control a big IK, or may strain muscles reaching over large tubes to paddle. For this boater, a K-1 affords plenty of space, even for gear.

Tube diameter also influences IK performance. Large tubes generate extra flotation, so an IK won't be swamped as easily in crashing waves. It's harder to tumble out of an IK with big tubes, and they also increase carrying capacity. So, an IK with large tubes may be just the ticket if you envision paddling large, fast rapids. Before buying, try to sit in the IK and work a paddle. Do it on the showroom floor if a "test-drive" or rental isn't available. IK tubes vary from eight to thirteen inches in diameter. Usually tube diameter is related to boat length—the longer the boat, the larger the tube diameter—but some K-1s are designed with the larger tubes. Generally, a K-1 will have tubes from ten to eleven inches in diameter, while K-2 tubes average twelve to thirteen inches.

In addition to the K-1 and K-2 ratings, official weight capacities are specified for some IKs. To determine how much gear the boat can handle, subtract your weight from the carrying capacity. For instance, a 150-pound boater riding in a K-2 rated at 400 pounds could carry up to 250 pounds of equipment. But you should exercise caution with this rule of thumb, because official limits on capacity are not specified for all IKs. Also, weight limits for inflatables have been exaggerated. This exaggeration derives from the practice of rating inflatables for use as emergency life boats and does not take into account the extra demands of whitewater. For instance, a raft rated as a ten-man can safely carry just five or six people in whitewater use. Overloading any whitewater boat is dangerous, because it greatly hampers maneuverability. Yet, IKs can carry amazing loads, and some perform nearly as well with a modest load as they do empty.

Choose from the smaller IKs for short trips, high-performance "hotdogging," very tight rivers, or for a petite paddler. For extended wilderness expeditions, stability in heavy rapids, cruising through wind, or for a large paddler, select a larger IK. Often, an intermediate size—around ten to eleven feet—is a good compromise for the average paddler.

OTHER DESIGN SPECIFICATIONS

Besides size, a paddler should consider how much the boat weighs. This is most important when the IK will be packed into a remote launch site—via backpack, pack animal, or bush plane—or carried as baggage on commercial airliners, which may have weight restrictions. Another situation that demands a lighter IK is a rugged float trip with several impassable sections, where the IK must be portaged around the dangerous waters. Lighter boats are popular with smaller paddlers, especially women, because they can handle launching and landing chores by themselves.

Most modern IKs are lightweight, between fifteen and forty pounds, with most models averaging about thirty-five pounds. Some design features, such as greater length and width or a self-bailing floor, will make the IK heavier. And, naturally, stronger IKs weigh more than flimsier models. Although some paddlers will find a lighter IK easier to maneuver than a heavier one, a few pounds here or there has little influence in how an IK handles once on the water.

Check IK specification sheets to determine how much the bow and stern of the boat curve up from the water, a characteristic that boaters refer to as "bow rise" and "stern rise" or kick. The amount of kick on an IK influences maneuverability in several ways. A shorter water line decreases the friction between the hard object—the boat— and the flowing current, allowing the IK to move with ease, turn quickly, and fit between most obstacles easily. Also, bow rise helps the IK climb over towering waves, but reduces the boat's stability, and catches more of the wind (a real annoyance on flatwater).

With less kick, more of the boat's floor is in contact with the water, creating additional resistance, and in effect slowing the boat. This drag is much less than a larger craft such as a raft would experience, but will make a low-profile IK slow when compared to a curvy, performance boat.

Having both ends of an IK elevated used to be one of the most important design features, because lift helped keep the boat from swamping—that is, filling up with water to the point where it began to wallow instead of float. However, with the advent of self-bailing IKs, kick has become a lesser concern. Consider kick in terms of how well an IK will turn (more lift) and how stable it will be (less lift). IKs designed for lakes and oceans should have little or no kick, because kick increases wind drag. On whitewater craft, bow and stern rise to pointy tips, a standard design feature that cuts down on spray intake and improves pivoting speed, but increases wind resistance.

Right above the kick line on many IKs are bow and stern covers, also called spray shields or splash guards. Like kick, these features were once deemed vital for the IK. The idea was that a partial deck would help repel errant waves, and it does in fact eliminate some water coming in over the ends, which helps keep your legs warmer when boating in cold water. In addition, a stiff splash guard on the bow helps keep the nose of the IK from diving too deep in a reversal, which can increase "play time" for the paddler, and aid in getting through whitewater upright. A splash guard also offers another handhold to grab during self-rescue.

On many older IK models, these covers—especially the bulky, inflatable ones—sometimes pose an obstacle to packing gear, so some boaters trim the stern spray shield back, or remove it entirely. Remember, however, that a stern spray shield can help hold gear tight inside the boat. Inflatable covers may prove annoying, too, because they add to the time it takes to inflate the entire boat, especially on a self-bailer, where they're not vital. Smaller shields remain a basic part of IK design because they strengthen and protect the sensitive area where the IK's twin tubes decrease in diameter and join, keeping the tubes in position during impact with waves.

Two air tubes are standard on every inflatable kayak design, and inflatable or foam floors provide additional flotation. Tubes and floors are constructed as separate compartments—known as air chambers—to increase safety. Multiple air chambers provide enough flotation that should one rupture, you can get the craft to shore and make repairs. Because of the inflatable's ability to bounce off obstacles that would destroy other boats, tube failure in open water is rare (even for cheap IKs). Accidents do happen, however, and it's nice to know that your boat won't let you down completely.

The Halkey-Roberts valve, ready to install. The cap prevents accidental discharge of air from the valve stem.

These tubes are inflated via metal or plastic valves. Poor valve design is worse than aggravating—it can be hazardous. Valve failure is extremely difficult to fix in the field. For expedition IKs, metal military-style valves are strong and dependable, although few IKs have them. They operate on a simple, practically foolproof system of the right hand thread: screw counterclockwise to open, clockwise to close. (Little arrows point out the correct directions for opening and closing the valves.) The only problems associated with metal valves are a tendency to stick, especially if screwed too tight (easily remedied with pliers), and difficult replacement (although the valves are so rugged, they'll probably outlast the boat unless severely abused). These valves are used in military assault rafts, as well as professional whitewater rafts.

Military-style valves come with a standard one-inch opening that accommodates most air pump nozzles handily. Most good IK valves will have one-inch openings, as well. Smaller valves may be found on inflatable spray shields or other parts. These take longer to inflate and require special adapters to operate.

A screw-in plastic valve. These are reasonably tough, but be cautious of cross-threading them.

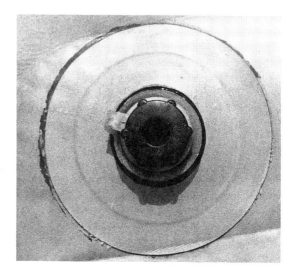

A plastic version of the military-style valve. These, along with the metal valves, offer virtually foolproof operation, with no parts to lose. They'll usually outlast the boat!

Plastic valves are coming on strong these days, with the Halkey-Roberts valve very popular for IKs and other inflatables. Manufacturers prefer the Roberts valve because it is easy to install. Many do-it-yourself boaters have learned to perform this surgery, too. To operate a Roberts valve one pushes in and twists on a center button to open the air chamber, then twists out and pulls to close. The design allows the valve to work one-way when closed, permitting air to be pumped into the chamber without the bother of opening the valve all the way for inflating, then madly rushing to close it before air escapes. This feature offers a tremendous advantage over the old-fashioned valves, which are often more difficult to use when inflating the boat, as air tends to leak out the valve during the pumping process unless the end of the air hose is held tightly to the valve.

Of course, there are drawbacks. Forcing the valve—often accidentally accomplished by novices who don't know how the valve works—can damage it. Although the Roberts valve is quite strong, military-style valves are tougher. Plastic versions of the military valve appear on some IKs. They are easier to turn than the metal versions, and seldom get stuck, but, naturally, are not as rugged. However, with reasonable care, quality plastic valves will last for years.

On cheaper boats, don't look for good, dependable valves. Instead, you'll find valves that are intended to be operated by mouth (an exhausting exercise). Also frustrating are valves closed by detached plugs, rendering an entire air chamber useless should the all-important stopper be lost. Plugs fastened by flimsy bits of plastic or string aren't much better—such retainers often break loose during normal wear and tear, and the plugs soon disappear. These may be replaced with Roberts valves for easier, more dependable operation. Screw-in plastic valves are fairly durable, but try to get the kind that don't need to be completely removed when adding air, like the Boston valve featured on Tahitis. Also, handle the screw-in plug carefully to avoid leakage caused by cross-threading.

Although multiple air chambers are important safety features, avoid excessive air chambers. Six or eight valves to inflate, instead of two or three, becomes tiring quickly, especially the tiny vinyl valves on spray shields, which usually must be inflated by mouth. On a good IK, there should be two strong valves, one on each side tube. An inflatable floor will add another valve. If the IK has a thwart (a cross tube positioned between the outer tubes to hold them apart), that will mean yet another valve. Most crucial are the valves on the side tubes; the loss of a floor or backrest isn't as devastating as the sudden collapse of a side wall. Get good, strong valves and you won't have to worry. All quality valves are recessed, to protect both the valves and the contents of the boat (including the paddler) from damage.

Valve placement is worthy of some thought, since a careful selection will save much aggravation later. Watch out for valves that might chafe when you are seated in the IK. Also, beware of valves that are in hard-to-reach places, like under a splash cover. Some valves are mounted in such awkward locations that you practically have to stand on your head to puff air into them.

Good, strong valves intelligently placed are one sign of quality workmanship on an IK. Another is the seam designs: how many seams are there, and how well are they sealed? Like valves, seams are crucial to the inflatable, because after all, holding air tightly inside the tubes is the name of the game. When inspecting IKs, check for strong seam tapes (bands of fabric applied over the seam joints to add strength and durability). Be wary of any IK that has sloppy seam tapes. Good seams are sealed by hand—one reason quality IKs cost more than cheap ones. The machine-sealed seams found on vinyl IKs aren't sealed with tape and are extremely difficult—many times impossible—to repair in the home workshop (or even in the factory) once they've ruptured.

Other considerations in IK seam construction are glue type and sealing system. Many inflatable boat owners prefer Hypalon coatings because they mistrust the strength of PVC adhesives, some of which break down after several years. Hypalon glues, such as Shore adhesive, are proven to last longer, while PVC has yet to stand the test of time. Also, the heat-seal process used frequently with PVC and vinyl IK construction isn't one hundred percent uniform, so a good bond is hard to achieve. (The use of internal air bladders is one way to circumvent these problems.)

Design details vary from one IK to the next. As manufacturers continually update and change their designs, more details are added. Manufacturers are just now beginning to listen to IK paddlers and respond to their needs. One important detail often overlooked is D-ring placement. D-rings, as the name implies, are metal rings flattened on one side to form a "D." D-rings are most commonly encountered in a creation known as a D-ring patch. First, the ring is fastened to a circle of coated fabric by gluing or stitching a pair of crossed nylon straps. Then the whole thing is secured to the boat with waterproof glue. D-rings are essential for a well-equipped

Metal D-ring patch on the bow of an IK, good for tying the boat up at night. Note "X" of webbing underneath the patch.

IK, and are used to tie equipment into the boat and to tether the boat when not in use. Although standard equipment on whitewater rafts for years, they are just beginning to appear on IKs. On day trips, it's possible to get by without D-rings, but they're indispensable for securing overnight gear. Lacking D-rings—or finding them to be improperly placed—paddlers can add their own. D-rings on bow and stern are useful for securing the IK to shore or a roof rack, or as grab loops for swimmers. D-rings allow cargo carried in the stern to be strapped down between opposite tubes, or between thwart and stern.

Concern for the boat's color may seem frivolous, but actually can be important in some cases. Bright warm colors—yellow, red, or orange—are highly visible colors, providing additional safety in big whitewater, where darker boats are difficult to see. (For the same reason, good life jackets usually come in warm colors.) From the cockpit of a search plane, a red IK is considerably easier to see than a green IK, especially in a pine forest. On the other hand, if you want to blend in, choose cooler colors, such as blue. Warm colors are a boon for color photography, and they're nice to look at and fun to ride in. Color choices are mandated by manufacturers, who often base their selections on economy—colored fabric coatings cost more—and practicality, as some fabric coatings are more easily colored or accept certain colors better.

SPINNING THE COCOON: FABRICS AND COATINGS

One of the most important decisions an IK buyer must make is choosing the fabric that forms the framework of his or her boat.

Inseparable from this decision is selecting a coating for the fabric. The strength and durability of an inflatable is determined by this combination of fabric and coating. What an IK is made of also affects the boat's handling and cost.

Contrary to popular belief, inflatables aren't made of plain old rubber. Construction of a good-quality inflatable—whether raft or IK—begins with a base fabric, usually heavy-duty nylon or polyester. The fabric base is then coated with PVC (polyvinyl chloride, commonly called vinyl), Hypalon, neoprene, or EPDM (a variation of neoprene). Less-durable inflatables are made of light-duty vinyl reinforced with a network of threads pressed into the material, and the really cheap models are made from uncoated, unreinforced vinyl. Each fabric and coating combination offers advantages and disadvantages; no one IK is perfect for every paddler and every use.

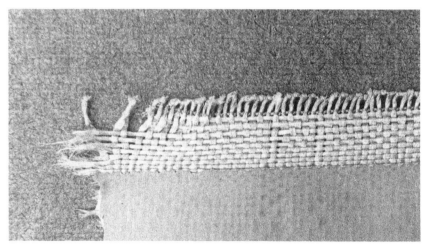

Fabric and coating work together. A coating of Hypalon was applied over the mesh of this heavy-duty nylon fabric, creating a tough, airtight seal.

Note that the terms PVC and vinyl refer to the same material. PVC serves as both a base and a coating in the construction of inflatables. To distinguish between the two uses, a reference here to "PVC" will mean a strong fabric *coated* with PVC, while "vinyl" will indicate PVC used as a base material, and not as a coating.

Consider, first, the strength of the base fabric. Fabrics used for inflatable boats are rated by "denier," a term of measurement that indicates a material's thickness and the weight of the threads used in weaving a fabric. In specifications for inflatable boats, base fabrics carry ratings such as 400 denier, 800 denier, or 1,000 denier.

In general, the larger the denier number, the stronger and more durable the fabric. This is why most good inflatable boat floors have higher denier ratings than the tubes: the floor takes a constant beating from the river, and also must be tough enough to withstand the boat's being dragged in and out of the water over hard surfaces. However, tube denier is important as well, because thin-skinned tube fabrics are more easily punctured than heavier versions, and a hole in a side-tube air chamber is much more serious than one in the floor. The minimum quality standard for an IK that can take on the toughest conditions is a combination of 840 denier tube material and 1,000 denier floor material. Extra layers of heavy material for the ultimate in protection against chafing and punctures are often offered as *wrap* floors. (To beef up a thinner-skinned model, a wrap floor can be added later by the do-it-yourselfer. See Chapter Two.)

Remember that denier alone does not determine the strength of an inflatable's fabric. Other factors to consider are the weight of the fabric, its tensile strength (how much force is required before it breaks or tears), and its resilience (will it stretch out of shape under moderate or heavy use?).

The buyer's selection of fabric characteristics, apart from denier, is limited. Manufacturers construct their inflatables from the fabrics and coatings they deem best, and finding out what kind of material they've used can sometimes be difficult. A quick rule of thumb is to consider the reputation of the manufacturer, and what fabrics and coatings they use to construct other inflatables, such as rafts. Good IKs should be made of fabrics that are the same kind, weight, and denier as those used in quality rafts. Generally, PVC-coated IKs are made with a polyester fabric core, which is more rigid than the nylon fabric used with Hypalon or neoprene coatings.

The quality of the coating is as important as that of the fabric itself. While base fabrics provide strength and tear resistance, coatings complete the package by sealing against air leakage. Good coatings are also abrasion-resistant, protecting the body of the IK much like the paint job on a car protects the metal underneath. Coatings must resist the ultraviolet (UV) rays of the sun, which can break down a weak coating, causing an inflatable to develop leaks.

Neoprene, the material used in wetsuits, was the standard inflatable coating for decades. It was used in military assault rafts because it was tough and reasonably priced. Then along came DuPont's Hypalon (featured in Hyside, Achilles, and Riken brand IKs), and PVC used as both a coating and a base material. Each is a premium-priced coating, very strong and durable. Over twenty-five different formulas for neoprene now exist. Because the best neoprene for inflatable boats—high-carbon black, like that used in tires—is usually weakened by the addition of color tints, boaters have turned their attention toward the more colorful Hypalon and PVC. Although neoprene can be colored, it usually remains basic black or gray, because dyes can reduce the high-carbon content necessary for providing UV resistance. Still out there, however, are a few die-hard neoprene boatbuilders. (Demaree makes the Dipper and other IKs from neoprene-coated fabrics, colored by a special process that reportedly retains the integrity of the original fabric). Hypalon is preferred over neoprene/EPDM by most boaters for its durability, as well as its attractiveness.

New on the IK scene (from AIRE) are separate air "bladders," airtight inner tubes of unsupported urethane that zip inside a tough outer shell. Thus insulated from rocks, these interior air chambers are difficult to puncture, and repair after a major rip is easy—just replace the inner tube with a spare. As whitewater boating increases in popularity, more miracle fabrics and coatings, and new ways of combining them, will no doubt be developed.

In the old-fashioned realm of vinyl IKs, remember that reinforced vinyl (such as Sevylor's "Sevytex") can withstand more pressure than plain vinyl. The hull will be more rigid, and the material less apt to stretch out of shape. Uncoated, unsupported vinyl is the least expensive—and least durable—IK material available.

Boaters and manufacturers alike continue to debate the pros and cons of the various coatings. Each manufacturer (or, more appropriately, importer/distributor, as most boats are assembled outside the U.S.) has its own formula for coatings as well—so, for example, you could encounter several different blends of Hypalon in your search for the perfect IK. How much abrasion resistance a Hypalon coating offers depends on the blending process employed by the manufacturer.

The toughness—and price—of a Hypalon-coated material is based on the percentage of Hypalon used in its manufacture; the greater the percentage of Hypalon in an inflatable's coating, the stronger, more durable, and costlier the boat. A coating of 25 percent Hypalon offers excellent durability, while an IK with 80 percent Hypalon coating is almost bomb-proof—although very expensive. Among top-of-the-line IKs, the choice is between Hypalon and PVC, both very tough coatings. Medium-priced IKs feature neoprene/ EPDM coatings, providing moderate durability, and the cheapest boats are made of unsupported PVC material, that is "vinyl." Reinforced vinyl employs a grid of threads pressed into the material for additional strength, limiting tears in boat fabric like rip-stop nylon does in sleeping bags. Unreinforced vinyl is the most prone to punctures and rips, even if touted by the manufacturer as "heavy duty" vinyl.

Hypalon is favored by the majority of inflatable users because of its excellent resistance to abrasion and the UV rays of the sun, which will degrade any coating over time. Hypalon-coated IKs are quite rugged and give many years of service. On the other hand, there are many devoted PVC enthusiasts who claim their coating is equally strong and resistant to UV rays. The chief advantage of the PVC-coated material is that the underlying fabric is polyester (not nylon), which, when combined with the PVC coating, produces a more rigid IK.

But in two areas, Hypalon seems to be superior: wrinkle resistance and ease of repair. Some boaters believe Hypalon has the edge in durability, as well. When a PVC inflatable is deflated and rolled up for storage, the fabric stretches and wrinkles, because it is stiffer and resists folding. PVC definitely has a "memory." In other words, it tends to fold in the same places each time it's rolled or compacted for storage. Repeated folding places stress on seams and fabric and, over time, can cause weak spots to develop. (Newer versions of PVC contain softening agents that are supposed to eliminate this tendency, but remember that chemical additives might evaporate out of the coating over time.)

If a PVC inflatable can be kept fully or partially inflated during storage, it remains a tough, durable craft. Because this coating creates less drag, IKs made from PVC are sleek "hotdogging" boats, great for playing in waves. For boaters who need to keep their boat rolled up, an IK coated with Hypalon or a related substance probably will prove more durable in the long run. Any inflatable will last longer and perform better if you can store it flat or partially inflated, rather than tightly rolled.

If you should damage your IK, or decide to customize the craft by adding D-ring patches or other glue-on accessories, Hypalon's superiority will become obvious. Patching Hypalon (and neoprene) is fast and uncomplicated. With PVC coatings, making repairs sometimes calls for mixing glue with an activator, a messy and time-consuming chore in the backcountry. Check the manufacturer's recommendations for repair procedures before you buy to determine how complex field fixes will be. (A product called Vyna-bond requires no mixing but hardens to a less-secure seal.)

Other basic differences arise when working with the two coatings: each requires different solvents, different glues, and different patch materials. In a pinch, Hypalon and neoprene/EPDM repair materials easily overlap. Incompatibility is seldom a problem until a flock of IKs on an expedition needs a repair kit. If two different types of coatings are present on the trip, the repair kit must contain twice as much glue and twice as much patching material, in addition to separate but equal amounts of solvent. And all paddlers must know how to patch their brand of boat, because the techniques differ. Life is simpler if all the IKs floating together are coated with similar materials.

HOW FABRICS AND COATINGS INFLUENCE IK PERFORMANCE

Beyond providing the fundamental integrity of an inflatable, fabrics and coatings—coatings in particular—also affect how an IK will handle on the water.

PVC coatings offer the most rigidity of all the coatings, with Hypalon a close second. This is an important IK design characteristic, because as a boat's stiffness is increased, friction is reduced and maneuverability is improved. Before good coatings came into widespread use, all inflatable boats were viewed as inherently inferior to hard-shelled craft, simply because it was nearly impossible to duplicate the rigidity of a boat made of wood, plastic, fiberglass, or aluminum with early inflatable boat technology. Inflatables were always a little on the squishy side, fine for bouncing off rocks but difficult to handle with precision. The reason was that the light-duty vinyl used in early versions of the IK, while cheap and easy to work with, resulted in a soft boat. The vinyl tubes just couldn't accommodate enough air pressure to make a more rigid IK. Plain vinyl also stretched out of shape, further decreasing the firmness of the boat. Floors sagged below the river's surface, increasing drag and decreasing maneuverability.

Lack of rigidity meant that smaller inflatables, like IKs, turned into mush under the force of a river. Naturally, staying in control under such conditions was difficult. In fact, just staying in the boat was a challenge because the early IKs lacked the stability and the "punching power" necessary to get through waves. They were also vulnerable to "tacoing," the dread condition in which the craft folds in the middle so that bow and stern meet, much like a taco shell. The paddler of a soft, wimpy IK exerts far less influence over what the boat is doing, and is at a much greater risk of going overboard or "flipping," than the paddler of a stiffer IK. Because of poor design and cheap materials, early IKs gained a bad reputation for being hard to paddle and control. As tougher raft coatings and fabrics began to show up in IKs, they underwent a transformation from "rubber duckies" to high-performance craft.

Rigid IKs are more pleasing to the eye, appearing more substantial. A rigid boat is a must for surfing waves and playing in holes (see Chapter Four). On a more practical level, stiffer IKs cut wind better and shed more spray than soggy craft. In addition to enhancing rigidity, the slick surface of a PVC coating allows an IK to slip more easily over the water's surface, giving PVC-coated craft the edge on quickness and maneuverability.

Construction is another factor that influences the IK's rigidity and performance. Solid floors of hard foam, tight inflatable floors, broad bottoms, and well-placed cross-tubes, thwarts, and seats all help maintain rigidity and thus stability, especially when negotiating heavy hydraulics. Keeping the air chambers inflated as tight as possible (without overinflating) vastly improves the performance of any IK on the market, and is essential for vinyl IKs, to give them some degree of stiffness.

Also influencing stiffness is the degree of airtightness provided by the coating. All inflatables depend on their coatings to keep air inside the tubes. Air pressure inside the chambers will vary according to outside environmental changes, however, regardless of how airtight the coating. Every boater will have to undertake the chore of adding additional air to, or "topping off," their craft every morning—and sometimes during the day, too—because the air pressure inside the chambers decreases from cool weather, cold spray, or even a change in elevation. A boat inflated with air at seventy degrees, then launched into forty-degree water, would soon become soggy from the change in air pressure caused by the drop in temperature. Boaters can either pull over and top off the chambers, or wallow through rapids, a risky proposition. Hot weather means just the opposite: air inside the tubes quickly expands, and a chamber could burst from the stress unless the valve is vented. This, of course, would necessitate topping off again once the boat had cooled down.

Although good coatings have not eliminated the environmental air pressure problem, Hypalon and PVC help cut down on the loss of air pressure. Many Hypalon boats can sit out overnight without losing air pressure, and so can some well-designed PVC craft. Neoprene/EPDM is fairly resistant to changes in pressure, while vinyl IKs, when tossed into the water, may respond like cornflakes doused with milk. A similar problem, pinhole leakage (air seeping through the fabric and coating), also results in a mushy boat but is stopped by a quality coating. Coatings that have developed pinholes from heavy use—or those that were applied thinly by the manufacturer—can be renewed by painting on another layer of coating.

SEATS AND THWARTS

Cross-tubes for IKs—which can be inflatable thwarts, rigid foam constructions, or air-filled "chairs"—provide more than comfort and back support for the paddler. These are an integral part of an inflatable's design, adding additional rigidity, and therefore stability, to the boat. Without some kind of cross-tube, the IK's side tubes may taco under the crush of heavy waves. Cross-tubes help the paddler make stronger strokes and maintain a consistent position. Without back support, a paddler could slide backwards and unbalance the boat.

Seats and thwarts also provide a barrier that keeps baggage from shifting out of place. The basic, no-frills backrest is just an inflated tube positioned crossways between the two outside tubes. Because the tube can't slip, it offers solid support for the paddler. However, tubes aren't very comfortable for long periods of time—they don't conform to the curvature of a paddler's back and they trap cold air against the paddler's body. Tubes are either integral (built-in, so they can't be taken out without dissolving the glue with a solvent) or moveable, with several positions that accommodate paddlers of different sizes. Integral tubes, called thwarts, are favored by commercial outfitters because constant seat adjustments are avoided—"one size fits all." Also, unlike other IK seats that are just tossed into the boat, thwarts can't be lost by careless renters. If you select an IK with an integral tube for a backrest, make sure the tube placement suits you.

Tube placement is often a problem with K-2 models. Long-legged paddlers, especially, may find the second tube in a 2-person IK useless. Tubes are extremely difficult to reposition, but it's easy enough to remove a second tube, using the correct solvent, to create more room in a K-2 for legs or cargo. (The surplus tube can be con-

The difference between a rigid foam seat, left, and an integral (fixed in place) thwart on the right. Note flip strap around the seat, necessary for holding it in place while running whitewater.

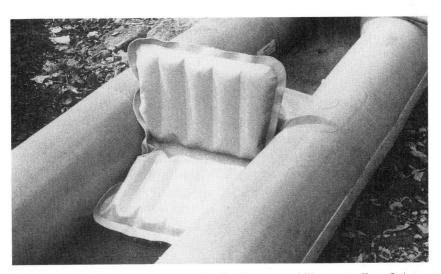

Riken's inflatable seat increases comfort for distance paddling, as well as fitting a smaller paddler more snugly in the IK.

verted into a lace-in thwart for an optional K-2, or chopped down into repair fabric.) Two-person models designed with moveable thwarts offer more versatility: the second tube can be removed for solo paddling, thus accommodating most paddlers and their cargo; reattach the thwart, and you're ready to paddle tandem.

The disadvantages of tube backrests can be overcome by keeping the tube tightly inflated and adding an inflatable or rigid foam seat over the tube or by placing a foam float cushion, such as a Type IV throwing cushion like the ones offered by Stearns, in front of the tube. These additions provide both insulation against the cold tube and increased comfort on long paddling days. For smaller paddlers in slightly oversized craft, cushions can be used to fill in the extra space, offering a more solid position for paddling. Some advanced paddlers prefer to sit on an elevated cushion, for increased paddling power, but beginners need to sit low for better balance. Once you've learned how to balance and brace, you can experiment with raising the seat.

Rigid foam seats are usually found on PVC-coated IKs. These offer excellent support for both paddler and boat. They don't have to be inflated, which saves time and trouble when rigging the IK, and they are very strong and durable. A foam seat will make the IK package a little bulkier, because the kind of foam used (rigid ethafoam, which is impervious to water) just won't fold easily. Like an air-filled tube, though, a hard foam seat can become a bit tiring after a long day and the addition of an inflatable seat or back cushion may be necessary to increase comfort.

Inflatable seats first appeared in the original IK, the Tahiti, and several IK designs now feature these triangular-shaped cushions. They offer wonderful comfort and support, and can be custom-inflated to suit each paddler's specifications. However, inflatable seats add little rigidity to the IK, especially bothersome with the Tahiti and other light-duty IKs, and they are extremely prone to punctures, although they're certainly luxurious while they last. Adding a cheap, Tahiti-style inflatable seat to a tougher boat with a hard tube seat has become a popular option. Tougher inflatable seats are made of the same rugged materials as quality IKs, and although not as comfortable, they last longer.

In most models, neither inflatable nor rigid foam seats are attached to the IK. This is an advantage in camp, where you can take the seat out of the boat for a wilderness easy chair. But loose seats are a nuisance when rigging the IK, because they take longer to position, and they need to be tied down, especially when boating in white-water. A tied-in seat stays with the IK even if it should flip and is one less thing to worry about. To circumvent this problem, IK designers are now creating built-in foam seats and some come with flip straps that not only keep the seat from jumping ship, but also help the paddler recover after an upset (see Chapter Five).

SELF-BAILING FLOORS

Nearly all of the top IK models are equipped with self-bailing floors. This feature offers tremendous advantages over the old-fashioned rubber ducky, elevating the IK from a toy to a serious whitewater boat. Self-bailers are safer, because although they may be momentarily swamped, the water will drain out quickly, enabling the paddler to remain in control. Self-bailing boats vary considerably in their ability to drain quickly. The best will self-bail in a matter of seconds. A small inflatable like an IK is easily rendered sluggish if a bathtubful of water is abruptly dumped inside it, and sitting in cold water is not pleasant. Scooping out surplus water is frustrating, time-consuming, and tiring.

Any boat, even a small IK, is very heavy once swamped with water; paddling is difficult, and the paddler could be injured during a close encounter with a swamped boat. If another rapid is fast approaching, the boat may not get bailed out in time, and emptying an IK loaded with cargo is even more difficult, because water tends to become trapped under the gear. Beyond the safety, comfort, and convenience they offer, self-bailing floors complement good IK designs, because the stiffer floors needed for self-bailing add to the boat's rigidity.

The major drawback to the self-bailing floors is their increased cost. A self-bailer (SB) requires more designing, more expensive

One of several popular patterns for drain holes on a self-bailing IK floor. This Momentum IK features two sets of eight round holes on bow and stern.

materials, and more work, all of which greatly increase its price. Unless the IK is destined for use as a sea kayak or flatwater boat, budget concerns are the only reason for selecting a model that is not self-bailing.

Self-bailing floors operate on two principals: elevation of the top part of the floor above the waterline, and the inclusion of holes in the bottom part that allow water to drain. Elevating the floor keeps water—all but minor seepage, that is—from leaking into the boat through the drain holes, and raises the seated paddler above the waterline. The only water that comes into the SB enters from above the waterline and exits quickly through the drain holes. In top models, the drain holes are large enough to empty the IK quickly. For example, an IK with four rectangular 2" x 5" drain holes offers a total "flushing system" of forty square inches, sufficient to empty the boat in seconds.

There are two methods of elevating the floor so that it empties itself of water. One features rigid ethafoam (in a two-inch-thick chunk, or in thinner layers), which is shaped to fit, then inserted into the bottom of the IK over a fabric floor. In most models, four drain holes are cut, one in each "corner" of the floor, at the bases of the bow and stern rises.

The other method of self-bailing relies on an inflatable floor. Instead of being installed above a fabric floor, an inflatable floor is usually laced with webbing into the sides of the IK. Occasionally, integral (glued-in) inflatable floors, with drain holes much like the rigid foam floors, are offered. To withstand the abuse they take, inflatable floors must be constructed of very rugged materials, or else installed as sub-floors, with a tough layer of coated fabric between the SB floor and the water. This is necessary to protect the inflated floor from punctures. Without full inflation, this type of self-bailer just won't work right.

The major difference between inflatable and rigid foam floors is compactability. Foam floors won't fold into a small bundle, while an IK with an inflatable floor will. (Also keep in mind that the construction of seats and spray shields influences compactability; for the smallest package, all parts of an IK must be able to flatten and roll up.) Despite the packing limitations, many paddlers prefer rigid foam floors because they really improve IK performance. The reason is that the foam floor is flatter on the water's surface than an I-beam inflatable floor, offering less resistance. The stiff foam responds to the paddle much like a hardshell boat, without the problem of

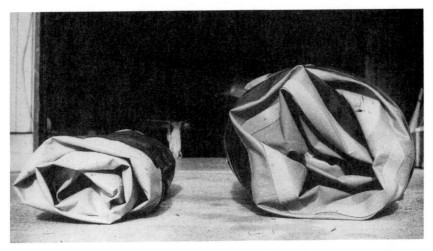

A comparison of the compactability of two IKs. The IK on the left is an all-inflatable, including the floor. The bigger bundle on the right is caused by an ethafoam floor, which creates more bulk.

dents or having to listen to the floor bang whenever a rock is encountered. Best of all, foam floors require practically no maintenance and will never rupture unexpectedly. Because of their stiffness, though, foam floors tend to be less comfortable for long-distance paddling. While inflatable floors offer more comfort, they tend to trap small amounts of water underneath your fanny. A small seat cushion is the answer in each case.

THE WHITEWATER PLAY BOAT

This is the river sports car, the inflatable version of the hardshell kayak. If you're interested in surfing waves on rivers and oceans, riding holes like a rodeo bronc-buster, or zipping from eddy to eddy in technical whitewater, the play boat is for you. There is no single design for an IK "hotdogger," but there are certain features that enhance a boat's ability to play.

First, you need a very rigid craft. Choose a PVC coating over a Hypalon coating—not only does a PVC coating produce a stiffer boat, it also lessens the boat's drag on the surface of the river. The polyester fabric used in most PVC-coated craft also adds to a boat's firmness, whereas the nylon in a Hypalon-coated IK tends to have more stretch. Also important is an all-ethafoam floor. Air mattresses can work loose while you're surfing a hole, while inflatable floors—no matter how rigid—won't surf as well as a foam floor. Forget vinyl

IKs like the Tahiti. They're too floppy for playing in the river. They can get you through the rapids, but that's about all. Even if you do manage to catch a surf (usually by accident), the mushy tubes may dump you overboard before you've had a chance to enjoy yourself.

A self-bailer is almost essential for surfing. Regular-floor IKs will quickly fill up with water and wash out of the hole you're trying to surf. The swamped boat will be ungainly until you can dump all the water out. On the other hand, it takes little effort to surf an SB, so purposeful stroking into a hole produces excellent results.

In addition, look for a play boat that will accept modifications that allow it to handle the sometimes-intense situations of surfing and hole-riding. Can you add braces to help yourself stay in? (Adding these to a vinyl IK would be very difficult in the home shop.) Is there a solid seat so you can brace yourself for hard paddling? (A squishy inflatable seat might not do the trick.)

A narrow IK will surf more readily than a wider one, but will dump you out more often. You may want to consider the very narrow, decked-over IKs that resemble fabric hardshell kayaks. Most are shorter than standard K-1s, as well. (Remember, the shorter the boat, the quicker it will pivot.) If you can find one of these, you'll

An example of a whitewater play boat. Look for a tough IK with a rigid foam floor. Also, this is where a self-bailer comes in handy!

have not only a play boat, but also a good boat for tackling steep, rocky rivers. Although none are on the new-boat market now, older models occasionally crop up.

Finally, some IK surfers prefer to have a bow spray shield to keep the nose of the boat from diving too far into the hydraulic.

THE VINYL IK

This boat is the exact opposite of the play boat. Many whitewater hotdoggers—both IK and hardshell paddlers—scorn vinyl IKs for their poor performance and lack of durability. Other paddlers are very enthusiastic about them, claiming they give a better ride in big waves, and that they actually rise over the high crests instead of crashing through. Again, the tremendous advantage of vinyl IKs is their low cost, an important consideration as the prices of better IKs keep rising.

Certainly, as a beginner's boat, the vinyl IK works well. It's important, though, that you understand their limitations. Vinyl IKs are a poor choice for rocky rivers, and shallow streams, where the IK's bottom constantly scrapes. Of course, they're not much for playing in holes or ocean surf. And, on extended trips, they won't carry as much gear or be as durable as the more expensive IKs.

The major problem with labeling the vinyl IK as a beginner's boat is that beginners make mistakes. Novices ram IKs over protruding sticks or crash into rocks while learning to handle their craft. All of this is hard on a vinyl IK, while a better quality boat would barely be affected by such mistreatment. Yet, there is a certain irony here. More experienced paddlers, who know how to read the river and control their boats, are able to greatly extend the useful life of a vinyl IK, but most veteran IK paddlers prefer the stronger boats that can withstand years of use and abuse.

Remember, if you choose a vinyl IK, treat it tenderly. Don't go dragging it over rough rocks or smooth boat ramps. These vinyl boats are lightweight, so there's no reason not to pick them up and carry them. Follow other recommendations in the next chapter, too, and you'll get many hours of enjoyment out of even the most modestly priced vinyl IK. River-trip outfitter Orange Torpedoes in Grants Pass, Oregon, claims their professional-model Tahitis have an average useful life of 300 to 400 hours each; this is excellent given the abuse that waves of novice paddlers inflict on these commercial vinyl IKs.

2

LIVING WITH YOUR IK
Maintenance and Accessories

Although modern IKs can withstand much more abuse than their meek predecessors and don't require much in the way of regular maintenance, a little care in handling your boat will ensure years of enjoyable paddling. Contrary to popular belief, more inflatables are damaged by rough handling than by rough waters; punctures occur more often as a result of carelessness than collision with obstacles. Therefore, most of the wear and tear that weakens your IK can be avoided.

After buying a new IK, assemble and inflate it indoors for inspection before taking it to the water. Be sure that all necessary parts are there. Leave the IK inflated overnight (out of range of curious pets or kids) so you're certain there are no pinhole leaks or other defects. If anything's wrong, don't use the IK or try to fix it—send it back to the dealer.

Exercise caution to avoid chafing the boat when transporting it to the water and back. An IK stuffed haphazardly into a trunk could spend hours rubbing against hard metal; the result is the same as if the boat had been pulled repeatedly over a jagged rock. To prevent damage during transport, many boaters keep their inflatable craft stowed inside a protective bag (canvas or other heavy-duty material works fine). Some sort of protective covering is especially important if your IK is to survive airport baggage gorillas. Should you desire to carry your boat atop your car, be advised that smooth straps are safer and easier to tighten than ropes, and that placing padding between the IK and hard surfaces will help lessen friction.

On the river, try your best to keep sand out of the inflatable. Sand is extremely abrasive—it is, after all, the key ingredient in sandpaper—

Prevent damage by lifting and carrying an IK—never drag the boat! (With a rigid IK such as this Padillac, carrying the boat with gear inside is OK.)

and constant rubbing of sand or gravel inside your IK will eventually wear holes. This problem is greatly lessened by the self-bailing feature, because most of the sand that finds its way into the boat washes back out again. Banishing sand from your IK, regardless of its breed, will help extend your paddling pleasure.

Most often, sand enters your IK attached to an object—your feet, or the bottom of anything that has been sitting on a beach. Before you enter the IK from a beach, sit on one tube and dip each foot into the water to wash off the sand. Dunk sand-coated equipment before loading, and check clothes for sand after sitting on a beach.

When coming ashore, don't jump out and drag the IK over a beach or boat ramp; pick it up and carry it. The boat is light, after all. Dragging an inflatable over hard surfaces will damage the floor; after repeated dragging, even the toughest floor will develop holes. Be particularly careful with inflatable self-bailing floors—if you puncture the floor, you'll have a bathtub, not a boat. Look out for unexpected hazards that can damage your IK: broken bottles or sharp rocks when landing, barbed wire and metal reinforcement bars ("rebar") along civilized reaches of river. Hone your river-reading skills so that you can quickly recognize and avoid natural obstacles like jagged snags protruding above the water. Also, use common sense when loading; don't store sharp or pointed objects (such as knives) inside the IK without adequate padding. Remember that avoiding damage is much easier than patching worn spots or holes.

After a trip, it's a good idea to wash your IK thoroughly inside and out, then let it air dry before you store it, especially if you plan to roll the boat up. If you roll up an inflatable with bits of sand or gravel, or other foreign substances, wedged between the tubes and floor, you're risking abrasion. Use a pressure nozzle to force-flush water into all the IK's nooks and crannies. If sand has worked its way below a removable floor, you'll want to pull the floor out to wash underneath. Drying the boat completely is recommended because inflatables stored wet will smell musty the next time out. However, don't set the IK into the sun to dry it faster. In fact, avoid storing any inflatable in direct sunlight whenever possible, as the sun's ultraviolet rays will eventually break down even the strongest Hypalon coating.

Unless you need a tiny package, there's no need to remove floors, seats, spray shields, and other accessories when storing your IK. Leaving these things with your IK lessens the chances of leaving behind something necessary for the next trip. Open all valves and wait for most of the air to escape (not all of it ever does, unless you use a vacuum cleaner or suction pump, and there's really no need to worry about this unless you're paying for freight by the square inch). When the IK is sufficiently flat, begin rolling at the end *opposite* of the main valves; this forces the rest of the air toward the openings. Larger IKs may need to be folded in half or in thirds (one tube folded inside first, then the other tube folded on top), and for an even tighter roll, fold the bottom third of this folded-tube package over the rest, then roll towards the valves. Remember that a PVC boat will last longer if stored inflated or flat whenever possible—and so will any other kind of IK, if you have the room—but if you store your IK inflated in a place where the temperature may fluctuate (such as a heated garage), let some air out of the chambers beforehand, to avoid overinflation.

Too much air can cause problems, especially for vinyl IKs. The thinner material just isn't built to be inflated tight as a drum; overinflation can stretch the vinyl and even burst seams. Extreme overinflation can also damage sturdier IKs—inflatable floors in particular. Overinflation most frequently occurs when an inflatable is left in the hot sun, not during storage in warm places. Expanding air trapped inside a tube or floor can easily rupture even the most expensive IK. Prevention is tricky; if you release the extra air as the manufacturers recommend, the boat will be a soggy mess when you put it back into the river, and will require topping off. Unless weather conditions conjure up images of Hades, a sensible precaution is to leave the IK in the water, where it will stay cooler than the surrounding air. Don't automatically pull the IK up onto shore and leave it there, or abandon it in the back of your car, especially when temperatures creep much above 85 degrees.

Some IKs feature pressure gauges that change color when the air pressure inside an air chamber is too high for the boat; also available are air pressure gauges that take readings from each valve. "Dump valves" that let excess pressure escape from an air chamber—great for those sensitive inflatable floors—are featured on some better IKs. Any chambers with black or dark colors absorb more heat, requiring more attention than lighter-hued fabrics (and black floors are almost an industry standard).

Check with the manufacturer of your IK to determine the proper air pressure and recommended method of inflation; some IKs can be pumped up with power inflators, while others may be damaged by the high pressure such pumps deliver. In general, though, quality IKs can withstand changes in air pressure better than wimpier versions can. Keep in mind that your IK must have sufficient air inside its chambers to deliver top performance. An IK that is not properly inflated will be sluggish, will wallow in rapids, and will quite likely dump you overboard the first chance it gets. Test the inflation by thumping the tubes with your hand. They should be firm and tight. Check each valve after inflating its air chamber to make certain it's tightly closed—otherwise you'll go crazy searching for a nonexistent leak.

Besides bursting seams, excessive heat may melt some IK materials, such as vinyl. Keep your IK away from fires and furnaces, and don't smoke in the boat! At the other extreme, some IK materials—PVC in particular—can become brittle in very cold conditions. It's best not to start unrolling your IK in a frigid garage; bring it inside and let it warm up first.

Certain substances may have a deleterious affect on some IK materials. In general, avoid contact with gasoline and other solvent-type substances. If you paddle through a suspicious substance, wash the IK clean at your first opportunity. Also rinse your boat thoroughly after paddling in salt water.

Then there are substances that are good for your IK's health. Chief among these is a product called 303 Protectant, which is recommended for both PVC and Hypalon-type IKs. This chemical soaks into the coating, and keeps it from breaking down over time.

Developed by the aerospace industry, 303 is also a UV inhibitor that can further extend the useful life of your IK. Because 303 is a slippery substance and may cause a paddler to slide out of the IK, apply it at the end of the season before you store the IK.

PATCHING THE IK

It's inevitable: inflatable boats get holes. Fortunately, patching an IK isn't difficult. Your IK should come with a complete patch kit (unless you bought it used). Most manufacturers recommend their own methods of patching, but the process is fairly standard for all inflatables.

In the field, if the hole isn't too substantial, you can make a quick, temporary repair with duct tape. Carry the heavy-duty kind; besides patching boats, it will repair broken paddles, ripped dry bags, and almost any other damaged item. In fact, river enthusiasts swear that duct tape can fix anything short of a broken heart. Make sure that the area to be taped is dry, and free of sand, dirt, or anything else that could interfere with adhesion. Of course, once at home (or in camp, if the hole is that serious), you'll need to effect a more permanent repair.

If the problem is a pinhole leak, you may have trouble finding it. In the field, you may choose to continue the trip, pumping air into the leaky chamber as needed to finish the day. Locating the source of a slow leak involves submerging the offending air chamber in water until telltale bubbles stream out. First, inflate the chamber to full pressure; this forces air out of the hole, making it easier to locate. Away from a handy source of water, apply soapy water (dish soap works fine) over the surface of the air chamber until you observe air bubbling out. Paddlers with sharp hearing can sometimes find these tiny leaks by listening for the shrill sound of air escaping, then homing in on it. If you don't find any obvious leaks, check around the valves—some may develop a slow leak over time. Once a pinhole has been discovered, mark the spot with a felt pen so you can find it again.

The Patching Process

After a hole has been located, assemble the items you'll need for patching before you begin. Read through the instructions in the repair kit you received from the IK manufacturer, if available, so the procedure and the recommended chemicals are familiar to you. Choose a well-ventilated work area for repairs. A warm area with a solid, level work surface is ideal, but in the field, you may have to make do with whatever's at hand. Deflate the damaged air chamber, so that more pressure can be exerted during the patching process.

First, cut a patch from matching material (floors usually require heavier fabric than tubes). The patch should be generously larger than the hole. Round off the corners of the patch, so there aren't any edges to snag and pull the patch loose. The inside of the patch and the area around the hole should be abraded with sandpaper to ensure better adhesion. Next, thoroughly clean the area to be patched with the correct type of solvent—usually, toluol or methyl ethyl ketone (MEK). Also clean the side of the patch that will be glued to the boat.

Position the patch over the hole, centering it, and trace a light outline of the patch. Apply a thin layer of glue to the patch and to the boat. Depending on the type of glue you're using, you may have to wait until the glue is tacky, almost dry, and apply a second coat, before sticking the patch down. Shore adhesive is commonly used for Hypalon/neoprene repairs. It forms a strong waterproof and airtight seal.

Apply the patch carefully, because you won't be able to reposition it. Lay the patched section over a hard surface, such as a table, rock, or board, and press hard. For best results, work the patch over with a roller (a repair tool somewhat like a miniature rolling pin) to thoroughly eliminate any air bubbles and weld the patch to the boat. Pressing with a smooth stone or paddle shaft will work in a pinch.

After the area is patched, let the IK sit until the glue is cured. The time required depends on the glue you use. It's always better to let the patch cure overnight, if possible, before adding air, even if your glue is supposed to dry in an hour. If you must use the boat before then, don't inflate the repaired chamber to full pressure. Don't take shortcuts when patching, because your IK will only be as strong as the patched area.

Long rips in the fabric present a special problem. During patching, the ends of the rip need to be joined. One solution is to stitch the rip together with needle and strong thread before applying a patch. Some boaters feel sewing further weakens the ripped area, and prefer to mate the edges with an inside-the-chamber patch before applying an external patch. This interior patch can be the same material as on the outside, or a piece of duct tape for a quicker repair. Severe damage may require sending the IK back to the manufacturer for repair—or replacement. Because of the inflatable's great resiliency, the chance of such severe damage occurring in anything but a vinyl IK is rare.

Inside the Repair Kit

On any trip lasting longer than a few hours, it's smart to carry along a full repair kit. (A roll of duct tape sealed inside a waterproof bag will suffice for shorter excursions.) After all, an IK is useless without air inside its compartments. The kit should include some kind of air pump for restoring injured compartments to full pressure.

Always carry patch material—extra fabric that matches that of your IK. Carry both floor and tube material and the appropriate glue and compatible solvent. For cutting patches, a sturdy pair of folding scissors works well. Add sandpaper, for abrading patches and work surfaces, swabs (paper towels, rags, etc.) for wiping on solvent, and small paintbrushes for applying glue. Include the manufacturer's repair instructions, if available.

Other useful items include a roll of duct tape, heavy-duty needles with strong, rot-resistant thread (handy for repairing not only long rips in boat fabric, but also tents and other equipment), a roller, a replacement button for a breakdown paddle and a small pair of pliers (for stuck valves, bent paddle blades, etc.). If your IK has Roberts valves, carry a valve-tightener, and perhaps a spare valve, just in case.

Gather these items in a sturdy, waterproof container, such as a small ammo can. Try to store containers of solvent and glue upright, to prevent leakage. Groups of paddlers might want to consolidate some items, but carrying a roll of duct tape in each IK isn't overkill: it's not impossible for a boater to become separated from the main group after sustaining damage.

CUSTOMIZING AN IK FOR COMFORT AND SAFETY

Few IKs come with all the extras, so to increase the safety and comfort of your boat, you may wish to add custom features. A simple strap around the middle of the IK will hold loose seats and cushions in place, and also serves as a flip strap, giving you something secure to hang onto should the IK overturn. Some paddlers disdain flip straps because they feel the straps cause drag on the bottom of the IK. The ability to scramble back into an IK quickly, however, overrides this minor performance interruption, especially for beginners—and when boating in big water. The strap should be attached in such a manner that it won't slide out of place or entangle you, yet offers a secure grip on the sides and bottom of the IK. Strapping in loose seats also means one less stray item for you to rescue. Remember, you have yourself, the paddle, and the IK to keep track of; swimming after a loose seat is a nuisance.

Ropes or cords strung along the sides of an IK should be avoided, because you can become entangled in them. A length of rope attached to a bow D-ring comes in handy for tying the IK up, but keep it coiled or stowed in a bag so that it won't come loose accidentally in thrashing whitewater. Some paddlers prefer a short cord with a clip on the end, which avoids the need to tie and untie knots every time you beach the IK.

While loose ropes present a hazard, something to grab onto after you've dumped out may be necessary, depending on the design of your IK. With many self-bailers, a swimmer can hold onto the lace-in floor, or put fingers inside drain holes. Climbing back into an IK with large tubes may require a flip strap or some other handhold, because you need leverage to haul your body over the bigger tubes. To increase the number of handholds, you can attach grab loops to bow and stern D-rings. If your IK doesn't have D-rings in the right places, you can buy D-ring patches and glue them where you need them.

Some enterprising paddlers make their own D-ring patches and save money. Use surplus patch repair material or similiar fabric, something compatable with your boat's coating. You can cut the circular patches yourself, or buy pre-cut circles. D-rings may be metal (make sure they're coated to prevent rust), plastic (must be very strong—avoid cheap ones), or plastic-coated metal. Select a heavy-duty nylon webbing that's the right width to fit inside the D-ring you're using. Cut two lengths of the webbing that are just shorter than the width of the circular patch. Place the two lengths in an X position inside the patch, crossing at the D-ring, and glue or sew them securely. (It's best to glue *and* sew, because the result is a far more durable patch.) To make the patch stronger and cleaner-looking, glue another circle over the patch, first cutting a hole to accommodate the D-ring.

D-rings are essential for strapping gear down, especially for wilderness expeditions. Although you can secure a gear bag by looping the strap around both bag and boat and cinching it down tightly, this arrangement can work loose in rapids, creating a potentially dangerous entanglement situation. You will need at least two, preferably four, D-rings in the stern compartment.

If you need to remove the second thwart from a K-2 to accommodate a large or long-legged paddler, or to create more space for gear, work the thwart loose by dissolving the glue with the correct solvent, a little at a time. Dissolve around the seam *inside* the IK, not the portion of the thwart that attaches to the boat (this will become your thwart "collar"). Keep pulling the thwart material away from the IK as you force solvent into the thwart's seams. Once the thwart is completely free, clean away all remaining glue with the solvent. To reinstall the thwart, add grommets along its outside edges and also at matching intervals along both sides of the thwart collars on the side tubes of the IK. When you want to use the second thwart again, lace both ends inside the IK, using a thin nylon webbing to bind the thwart's edges inside the collars. Or, if you don't need the second thwart, put it aside to use as extra repair material. You may also salvage the valve from the thwart to use as a replacement, for repairs, or for improving the air intake of an air mattress.

Again, avoid rigging loose lines or ropes on an IK, and—except for ocean and lake boating—never attach yourself or your paddle to the boat with anything! In rough waters, it's possible to become entangled in such a line and be trapped under water (see Chapter Five).

Paddlers tackling rough water, where staying in the boat is important to their safety, have begun to add thigh braces made from straps or chunks of ethafoam. These braces allow you to reach further with the paddle, and stabilize your lean, so that you won't fall out as easily. (Thigh strap braces are employed by some canoeists for the same reasons.) The principle of the braces is simple: you tuck your thighs underneath them and flex your muscles or bend your legs to hold yourself in place. Should your legs relax or straighten out—as they would in a flip—you aren't held inside. Once foam braces are added to the IK, however, it's very much a custom boat, and won't fit anyone who isn't the same size. Foam braces are glued onto the side tubes above your thighs, positioned so that when you flex your thigh muscles, they bump the braces. Braces from webbing material are available as factory additions on IKs made by AIRE. They're sewn onto the boat during its construction. These are more adjustable than foam braces, and are considered better by experienced AIRE paddlers. If you don't want to use them, just tuck them out of the way. Although the braces are specifically designed for the AIRE Lynx

PVC-coated IKs, a kit for adding them to other IKs is also available from the company (see Appendix for manufacturer's addresses).

Some IK paddlers are also experimenting with carving footholds into ethafoam floors, or installing foot braces (in the form of ethafoam blocks) into the bows of their IKs. The idea is to increase the likelihood of your staying in the IK without risking entrapment should the boat flip. Make certain that any additions don't hamper your ability to escape from the boat if it overturns.

Finally, to extend the life of IKs made of less-durable materials, add a wrap floor (a second layer of fabric glued over the floor and lower side tubes) or an additional layer of coating, which brushes on like paint.

CONVERTING YOUR IK INTO A SELF-BAILER

Still on the market are many well-constructed and some lower-priced IKs that were made before self-bailing floors became standard. Economy-minded paddlers can improve the performance of these IKs by converting their standard floors into self-bailers. (See illustration.) First, cut four drain holes into the attached floor, which will become your subfloor. (A popular design is four 2" x 5" holes at the four corners where the IK's "kick" begins.) Glue reinforcing material around these drain holes to strengthen them, and then carve a sheet of ethafoam to conform to the interior of your IK. The edges of the foam should be carved at a downward slant, to allow full drainage. At this point, you can either carve out four openings on the foam sheet that match the drain holes on the floor, or carve a bunch of smaller drains.

The thickness of the ethafoam needed to self-bail an IK depends on the boat's construction and the body weight of the paddler. Heavier people will need a thicker layer underneath them, while lighter people won't require as much to achieve the same effect. Generally, four to six inches of elevated floor is necessary to achieve the self-bailing effect. Elevating the inside floor *above* the outside water level is the secret to creating a self-bailer. A removable air mattress floor is standard in some IKs and available as an accessory for others. These can be combined with two inches of carved ethafoam to make a very effective self-bailer. (The air mattress alone doesn't make a good self-bailer because incoming water gets trapped between the mattress and the floor material, causing the floor to drag and the boat to be unresponsive until bailed.)

To turn an older IK into a self-bailer: first, cut four drain holes and glue reinforcement material around the holes. Then cut an insert for the floor (measuring the inside of the IK), and carve matching drain holes. Slant the sides of the foam insert so water will drain off the floor into the holes, and you're ready for serious whitewater.

For most IKs with air mattress floors, two to three inches of etha-foam above the floor is sufficient. A single chunk of one or two inches is easier to acquire and carve than are several layers of thin-ner foam, although the thicker sheets are less flexible, and therefore harder to fit inside an IK. Be sure, when assembling a homemade SB, that the subfloor lines up with the drain holes in the original floor—this speeds up the self-bailing process.

It's even possible to convert a vinyl Tahiti-style IK into a "semi-self-bailer." Sevylor's "professional" heavy-duty model comes with a hole cut in the stern, where the rubber D-ring attachment is sup-posed to be. This hole helps drain the Tahiti, cutting down on the bathtub effect. The bailing, however, is neither quick nor efficient, and the boater is expected to assist the process by swirling the IK around, using centrifugal force to propel water backwards towards the hole (the "spin-dry" technique). The professional model is avail-able only from Orange Torpedoes (see Appendix).

Many inventive paddlers are thinking up new ways to convert various old-style IKs into self-bailers. Remember the basic formula: elevate the floor and provide reinforced drain holes. Some discour-aged paddlers of inexpensive vinyl craft are installing carved sheets of ethafoam, sometimes with drain holes cut, and are leaving the floor deflated. The result is a more rigid boat that responds better without tacoing. Despite the fact that vinyl IKs are difficult to work with in the home shop, this method is worth trying, especially with a salvaged piece of ethafoam. Should you ever destroy the floor of your non-self-bailer (or acquire one already done in), converting it to a self-bailer could save the boat's life.

PADDLES FOR IKS

The double-bladed kayak-style paddle is universal for propelling the IK. Canoe-type paddles with single blades are inadequate in all but a few of the really long IKs, which are more like inflatable canoes than kayaks. You need to stroke on both sides of the IK for maximum efficiency because inflatables lack the keel that makes a hardshell boat track. And, usually, paddlers in IKs sit too low for effective stroking with single bladed paddles. Some IK paddlers use them anyway, especially the bow person in a K-2. Don't bother with motors; nearly all IKs are too small for power propulsion, and besides, the best wilderness paddling waters usually forbid motors.

Standard whitewater kayak paddles are seven feet long, sometimes less—too short for inflatables. For efficient, comfortable paddling when sitting low in an IK, you need a paddle that's eight feet long. Unfortunately, most top-quality paddles that are made to last are designed for hardshell use, and some may be too short for use with inflatables. (Note that some advanced IK paddlers prefer to sit higher and use a standard hardshell kayak paddle—not recommended for beginners.) But there are some good choices for IK paddlers now on the market.

Eight-foot, double-bladed break-down paddles made of aluminum and covered with plastic, such as the model manufactured by Carlisle Paddles, are ideal for paddling IKs, especially for novice paddlers. In addition to offering easy storage and transport, the paddle's break-down design allows you to choose whether or not to feather the blades. (Feathered blades are set at right angles to each other). Also, should one blade break, you needn't throw away the entire paddle—just replace the bad half. The joints of break-down paddles are subjected to heavy stress, so make sure the one you select has reinforcement in this area. During heavy use, aluminum paddle shafts have a tendency to flex, and they can develop bends that cut down on paddling efficiency, so experienced paddlers may want a better-quality paddle. If so, the break-down makes a good spare.

Paddles for whitewater use need to be strong, yet light. You'll be holding the paddle all day in your hands, so avoid really heavy paddles. A paddle should be comfortable to hold. Look for a smooth shaft that won't blister your hands as you rotate the blades during paddle stroking. Wide blades deliver more power for each stroke you take and are suitable for all conditions except in strong headwinds, when the blades may slow you down. Drip guards, little plastic cups that keep water from dribbling down the shaft toward your hands, are nice to have but not essential.

Favored by traditionalists, wooden paddles are a delight to use. They're beautiful to look at, light to hold, and they have a wonderful feel in the hands. However, they break much more easily than paddles constructed of synthetic materials, and few wooden paddles are available in the longer length needed by most IK paddlers, unless you have them custom built. As inflatable kayaking grows in popularity, though, more manufacturers are responding to the demand and coming out with longer paddles. The chief drawback to wooden paddles is the maintenance required to keep them in good working order—they can warp if not taken care of properly. Wooden paddles need to be refinished on a regular basis and carefully stored away from moisture.

Paddles designed for sea kayaking sometimes work for inflatables. For most paddling, you'll want wider blades than some sea kayak paddles offer—the more blade surface, the greater power in each stroke. (Narrower blades are designed to cut wind resistance, important in open-water paddling but not on most rivers.) Consider the paddle's intended function: one that's too long will be awkward in tight stretches of whitewater and difficult to control, but it might be ideal for paddling against the wind on a lake, where the leverage gained from extra length aids your cause. If you paddle both flat water and whitewater, you might want two paddles of different lengths. Some paddles are available with extensions so that one paddle will work for varied water conditions.

Paddles to avoid include the flimsy types sold in discount stores next to the vinyl IKs—even the most modestly priced inflatable will operate better with a quality paddle than with a piece of junk. Beginners are wise to stick with flat-bladed paddles, leaving "spoon" blades, which are curved on one side, for later. With a spoon-bladed paddle, the power (curved) surface must always be in proper position to be effective; in whitewater, where things happen fast, an inexperienced paddler can easily get the blade surfaces confused. For experienced paddlers, the curved surfaces of spoon-bladed paddles minimize splashing, and increase the efficiency of each stroke, particularly on flat water.

Several methods exist for protecting palms from the stress of the rotating shaft. Simplest is to wear gloves: neoprene or other warmth-retaining handgear in cold weather, leather or other protective covering in warmer conditions. Choose gloves that pad the palms where the paddle may chafe, such as fingerless weightlifting gloves. Special paddling gloves are available, also. During a long trip, carry adhesive tape for protecting any blisters that develop— use duct tape if nothing else is available. Foam grips that fit over the shaft are available, and some boaters use grips made for bicyclists. If the shaft is new and slippery, a layer of duct tape, although ugly and hard to remove, offers a degree of hand protection and friction.

Your paddle is your IK's sole means of propulsion, so treat it kindly. Don't push off rocks with your paddle blade or use it as a lever to pry a stuck boat free. Avoid using your paddle to splash others during water fights—some aluminum paddle blades and shafts will bend from such abuse.

Paddle repair in the field is difficult, but not impossible. Use a spare paddle, if one is available. If you've broken a blade on a break-down paddle, only the broken half needs to be replaced; save the other half. The most common site for failure in break-down paddles is the joint that joins the two shafts. Should a push button break, the entire button assembly can be replaced, if you're carrying a spare. If not, duct tape wrapped tightly around the shaft may hold the two shaft pieces together. In case of complete joint failure, find a sturdy stick or two, position them over (or inside) the broken joint, then duct tape the entire affair. Bent paddle shafts or blades can be straightened by applying weight and force; stand (carefully!) on them and pull back into shape.

Paddle leashes, short lengths of light line (such as thin shock cord), are commonly employed by sea kayakers and lake boaters to keep their paddles from straying, but they should never be used in whitewater, due to the risk of entanglement.

SELECTING THE PROPER PFD

Just as essential as your paddle is your personal flotation device (PFD), or life jacket. In a small boat like an IK, you should never venture away from shore without wearing a proper PFD—it's dangerous as well as illegal. Today's modern life jackets are very safe, quite comfortable, and even stylish, so there's no excuse for not wearing one. In particular, you need a PFD in whitewater, because the aerated froth churned up by rapids is considerably less dense than flatwater and provides little support for a swimmer. Every year, scores of boaters are drowned because they refused to wear life jackets—don't become a statistic.

PFDs are rated Type I through Type V by the Coast Guard, according to how they are used. The only types for serious consideration by

Two good PFDs for IK paddling. The left is a Coast Guard Type III with foam ribs, plastic zipper, and waist belt. On the right is a Type V with solid foam inserts and plastic Fas-tex buckles.

IK paddlers are the Type III and Type V. The Type II, shaped like a horsecollar, is uncomfortable to wear, offers too little flotation for whitewater, and can be yanked off by strong river hydraulics. The Type I, typically a huge, kapok-filled device, known as a "Mae West" for the buxom profile it presents, offers high flotation for heavy water but is too bulky for IK paddlers. Kapok-filled PFDs are easily damaged; the flotation material is enclosed in a plastic membrane, and if the membrane is ruptured, the filling absorbs water, rendering the jacket useless. Some Type Is now feature closed-cell poly foam, which is tougher than kapok filling, but more rigid (and therefore bulkier). The same high-flotation offered by the Mae West is now available in the more dependable Type III and Type V jackets that use softer closed-cell foam, so there's really no reason to bother with a Type I for IK boating. The Type IV is a throwing cushion and is totally unsuited to IK boating, except for use as a seat or backrest.

For safety in an IK, you'll need a Type III or Type V PFD that is filled with closed-cell foam, a special type of foam that won't absorb water, yet offers reasonable comfort. The best life jackets are made with ensolite foam, which is soft and conforms to the body's contours for comfort. Type III PFDs, usually shorter jackets with foam flotation "ribs" rather than "slabs," are designed for canoeists and kayakers who require maximum freedom of motion. The Type V category covers special designs for whitewater, generally with commercial raft passengers in mind. These jackets offer greater flotation and safety than the Type III, but tend to be bulkier and more restrictive.

When choosing a PFD, favor safety over comfort. One special requirement to keep in mind, however, is that because of your sitting position in the IK, some long-waisted jackets may prove restrictive, especially for longer excursions. PFDs designed for hardshell kayakers often have extra flotation in pads below the waist tie, which are flipped up for paddling. The amount of flotation you require depends both on your experience and the kind of water you'll be floating. A beginner will be better off with a high-float jacket—at least twenty-two pounds of flotation—because it provides more security. A veteran paddler accustomed to swimming in heavy water may not require as much protection. For trips in calm waters or on easy rivers, a "shortie" Type III offers a good measure of safety and the advantage of unrestricted motion. In Class III and IV whitewater, wear a Type V or a high-float version of the Type III.

Quality life jackets aren't inexpensive. Be prepared to spend $60 or more, and feel good about spending that money—it's cheap life insurance. Good safety features to look for on a PFD include secure fasteners (most IK paddlers prefer plastic Fas-tex buckles or zippers to metal snaps that your hands can bang against), and a collar or head flap (flotation behind the head helps support an injured or panicky boater). There should be sufficient buckles and straps to secure the jacket firmly about your body (Type IIIs may need crotch straps in heavy whitewater). You'll want to wear the PFD snugly enough to keep it from riding up over your head, so make certain you purchase a jacket that fits you. Most Type IIIs are sold by chest sizes, while the majority of Type Vs are "one size fits all" and usually true to the claim. Fit is important to safety, especially for children and petites (under 100 pounds), and short-waisted paddlers. An ill-fitting jacket can easily slip over the head, even in moderate white-water. Always fasten *all* the buckles, zippers, and waist-ties when you put the life jacket on—never wear the PFD loose or open in the front. And pull the side adjustment straps down *snug*.

A good PFD will give you years of protection if treated properly. Don't use your life jacket as a sitting cushion—quality PFDs are rugged, but not indestructible. After each trip, hang the jacket on a plastic-coated hook (never a nail, which could snag the jacket when you retrieve it). Hang up the PFD when it is wet to prevent the material from mildewing. Clean your PFD carefully, following man-ufacturer's recommendations, using a mild soap so as not to harm the flotation foam. Also, be careful with your jacket in transit—don't tie it on the outside of a moving vehicle where the wind will whip over it, or where it could blow loose. Make a habit of clipping your life jacket down when you take it off, so wind or water won't carry it away.

AIR PUMPS

IKs may appear small enough to inflate by mouth, but not even the most long-winded politician has enough hot air to inflate an IK to full pressure. Some kind of inflation device is therefore necessary. Even if you leave your IK inflated all the time, you'll still need a pump for emergencies. And, if you use an air mattress in camp, you'll find that using a pump is much easier than giving mouth-to-mouth resuscitation to your bed.

Three basic kinds of air pumps. On the left is an up-and-down hand pump, on the right a foot pump. Below is an electric Dowco pump that runs off a car battery.

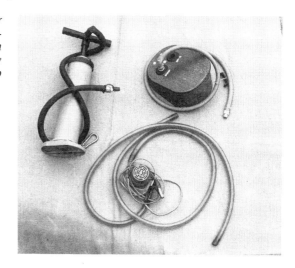

A heavy-duty foot pump works quickly without power. Because a foot pump uses your body weight for leverage, it's the most effective manual pump available.

There are three types of pumps: foot pumps, hand pumps, and power inflators. For both convenience and efficiency, a foot pump is superior for IKs. By using the weight of your entire body to stomp on the pump, you increase your mechanical advantage, making the chore easier. It takes about five minutes to inflate an IK with a good foot pump. Quality foot pumps will be heavier—and last longer—than cheap ones. You may want to have a good, heavy pump for initial inflation and a smaller one to carry for emergencies.

Power pumps operate off either 110-volt household current, or a 12-volt car battery. While you *can* plug a 110-volt Big Blower into a generator and whomp up IKs in seconds at the launch site, it's overkill unless you have dozens of IKs to inflate, or big rafts accompanying the party. These blowers put out high volume that can damage weak vinyl IKs, so exercise caution.

Inflators such as the Dowco or LVM that run off a car battery are handy for a large party. These fill IKs quickly and won't overinflate them. You may want to leave your car running while you inflate the boats, so you won't drain the battery.

Up-and-down hand pumps require much more effort than foot pumps, but are cheap and compact. They make good emergency pumps. Also available are mini-pumps such as the model made by Intex; they're great for filling tiny air valves such as those on Tahiti spray shields. Some IK manufacturers include an air pump with their boats, but with most, you're on your own.

Whichever type of pump you select, check the fittings at the end of the air hose to be sure they match the size of your valves. Pumps designed to inflate air mattresses usually won't fit the standard one-inch IK valves, but adapter nozzles for the air hose are available. If you must use a pump with a nozzle that doesn't fit, improvise a gasket (an article of clothing or a bandanna works well) to close off the air leakage.

ACCESSORIES FOR IK PADDLING

Nearly all hardshell kayakers, and a lot of whitewater canoeists, wear special helmets when paddling. Hardshell boaters need helmets because when they get tossed out of their boats, there is always a hard surface (the boat) near their heads. Even on the easiest waters, hardshell kayakers can flip over, and their boats are designed to hold them in place—even if they're upsidedown with their heads bumping over the river bottom. So, they wear helmets. These days, IK paddlers are beginning to wear helmets, too, mostly because they are challenging tougher, rockier rivers where helmets provide an important extra measure of safety. It's tough to swim or perform self-rescue after clunking your head on a rock, even if you're still conscious.

On easier waters, helmets aren't needed for IK use, but when you start running more difficult water, a good whitewater helmet could save your life. Buy a helmet that's designed for whitewater—don't try to use a football or cycling helmet. As for fit, the helmet should be snug, but not so tight that it causes discomfort. The protective internal suspension is usually foam, but cheaper versions will have plastic strapping. The helmet must have a chin strap to hold it in place. Whitewater helmets are designed with ear openings so you can hear upcoming rapids or a companion's warning shout.

Rope lines on bow and stern are handy for securing the IK to shore, for towing, or for tying up to another boat. Some boaters favor clip lines, a short length of line with a metal clip that fastens without fancy knots. If you add ropes to your IK, be sure to keep them safely stowed away in such a fashion that they won't come uncoiled on the water (secure them in small bags, bound with elastic cord, or with one end of the line wrapped around the coil). Loose lines aren't just inconvenient, they're dangerous, because should you be dumped from the boat, you can become entangled in them and drown (see Chapter Five).

On any expedition, at least one boater in the group should carry minimum safety equipment: first aid kit, repair kit, carabiners for boat rescue, and a throw-bag filled with rope for rescues or lining rapids. Boaters who are out often like to wear whitewater safety knives. Two musts for river knives: rust-proofing and easy one-handed operation (in case one arm is entangled). The parachutist's line cutter slices through ropes quickly, but a paddler's knife must also slash boat fabric in emergencies, something the line cutter won't do effectively. Most kayakers wear their knives on their PFDs so they're readily accessible—not just for a macho display. Also, attaching the knife upside-down aids in unsheathing it. A serrated edge on the knife is more efficient at sawing ropes, and a double-edged knife is better than a single cutting surface. For more information on safety gear, see Chapter Five.

CURRENT FASHIONS: CLOTHING FOR IK BOATING

When selecting clothing for IK boating, keep in mind that IKs are *wet* boats. Even in a self-bailer, waves wash over the sides and douse you, and some water will enter the floor through the drain holes. Feet get soaked from this, as well as from climbing in and out of the boat. Most good paddling waters are cold, too, and the combination of cold and wet can prove dangerous to an unprepared boater. Whenever the water temperature and air temperature add up to less than 100 degrees, you definitely need the protection of a wetsuit or drysuit to prevent hypothermia, the dangerous lowering of your body's core temperature that can cause death. If the wind is blowing, you'll need nylon outerwear for additional protection against the wind-chill factor. If rain threatens, waterproof clothing will keep you warm while paddling or in camp.

Avoid floppy clothing—ponchos in particular, because these make for cumbersome swimming and can be dangerous if they get caught on equipment or branches. Also, don't wear clothing over your PFD—always wear the PFD on top.

For serious IKers, a wetsuit or drysuit is a good investment for years of safe, comfortable paddling. These protective outfits allow you to start your paddling season early and keep on paddling long after the crowds have gone home for the summer. To improve your skills, and progress to tougher paddling, you'll want to be out on the water as often as possible. With protective clothing, a little bad weather won't force you indoors.

Wetsuits made of neoprene are the original cold-water garment, first worn by scuba divers. These early suits made the wearer look like a frog and walk like Frankenstein, due to the thick fabric necessary to keep deep-water divers warm. Now, with the soaring popularity of water sports such as boardsailing, a wide variety of colorful, stylish wetsuits are available. For most IK boating, an eighth-inch-thick fabric is plenty thick to keep you warm. Protecting the torso is most important, so most wetsuits are of the "Farmer John" type, sleeveless one-piece affairs with a zipper down the front for entry and exit. Boaters choose between ankle-length and short-legged versions, depending on how cold-blooded they are. To increase the warmth this type of wetsuit provides, you can wear a paddling jacket, polar fleece pullover, wool sweater, or polypropylene underwear top over the wetsuit. Add wool socks or wetsuit booties and gloves, and you can withstand all but the most severe conditions. For really cold water and air temperatures, a wetsuit jacket is necessary.

What you wear underneath the wetsuit is a matter of personal preference. Some paddlers—both men and women—find that any kind of underclothing chafes below the skin-tight surface of the wetsuit, so they don't wear a stitch underneath them. Others, many women in particular, prefer to wear something like a nylon bathing suit or running-type clothing underneath. (Cotton underwear isn't bad underneath, but it never dries out.) The advantage of wearing a bathing suit-type outfit is that you can partially or totally remove the wetsuit without exposing anything in particular. This is a real advantage at the end of a day trip, when you are "running the shuttle" back to the launch site—who wants to drive or ride in an icky wet rubber suit? Also, if the weather turns hot, you'll roast in a wetsuit, and it's nice to be able to take the suit off.

Wetsuits require some care to keep them wearable. After each trip, turn the wetsuit inside out and rinse it thoroughly with clean, cold water (best done in the bathtub, especially with one of those Shower Massage detachable sprays). Booties need a good rinse, too. Otherwise, both you and the suit will soon begin to smell like an old goat. Special soaps for cleaning neoprene wetsuits are available.

Because they fit so snugly over the body, it's not uncommon to tear the neoprene fabric when struggling to pull a wetsuit on. And after numerous trips where you scramble through the bushes to scout rapids or whatever, rips inevitably develop. These damages can be repaired with special wetsuit glues, available where you bought the wetsuit.

If you won't be needing a wetsuit all the time, or aren't sure if you want one, they can be rented at very reasonable prices. Try a commercial whitewater outfitter or a local dive shop.

Wetsuits keep you warm by absorbing some water and holding it close to the body, where it is heated by your body warmth. They don't really keep you warm *until* that first dousing. Drysuits, on the other hand, are wonderfully luxurious garments designed to keep the cold water from ever making contact with your body. You can wear them alone or with cuddly warm fleece undergarments in really cold conditions. Of course, they're not inexpensive, but for the ultimate in paddling comfort, a drysuit can't be beat. Remember, though, that drysuits are easily punctured (rendering them useless) when scrambling around during scouting.

Some drysuits have built-in boots, others require footwear. Proper footwear is important, in all paddling conditions, to protect the feet from sharp rocks while wading or taking an unexpected swim. Wetsuit booties made of neoprene help keep feet warm when wading in cold water. Get the kind with sturdy soles so your feet will be protected from gravel and rocks—thin soles are miserable after a hundred yards of boulder hopping, and changing shoes every time you want to scout a long rapid or hike up to a waterfall is a bother. If it's really cold, wear wool socks under the booties. Alternatives include "water slippers," like the Nike Aqua Sock, or an old pair of tennis shoes that you don't mind getting soaked. Thongs are great for camp wear, but are unreliable as river wear, as are open-toed sandals; these can easily fall off, inviting injury to the feet. Special river sandals, produced by Teva and other manufacturers, are designed to stay securely on the feet and are self-draining, allowing your feet to dry periodically during a day of constant inundation from spray.

Paddle jackets are garments with wrist seals designed to keep water from dribbling inside your sleeves as you paddle. Shedding both spray and wind, they're great over a wetsuit, or as a warm top to accompany a pair of shorts in milder conditions. With a paddle jacket, you can save the warm fleece top for camp wear. These are available from most river equipment suppliers, along with nylon pants made for paddling. Many boaters like to wear their raingear, which sheds spray and keeps wind off and body heat in. The only problem is that the raingear wears out more quickly than gear that is designed for whitewater conditions. Raingear that loses its water repellency can be renewed with a fresh coating applied at home.

For moderate conditions, select clothing that keeps you warm even when wet, or clothing that absorbs little water: wool, polar fleece, fiber pile, Capilene, and polypropylene. On warm days, nylon running shorts or swimsuits will be suitable. Also popular are special river-runner's shorts—such as those by Patagonia, Sierra Designs, and Schwabbies—made of supplex for quick drying. Avoid cotton—it stays wet all day, giving your skin a clammy feel even on a balmy afternoon. Even cotton underwear soon becomes uncomfortable—when paddling, most people are more comfortable in nylon shorts with built-in liners. Except for sun-sensitive people who can use light cotton clothing to cover up on hot trips, save the cotton underwear and sweats for camp wear.

If you paddle in shorts, don't forget the sun lotion. Water magnifies the sun's damaging rays, causing severe sunburns even on moderately sunny days. Sun screen with a protective factor between eight and thirty is best, depending on your skin type. Make sure to get the water resistant variety, too. Sitting flat in an IK, your lower legs get much more sun exposure than you'd expect, so keep applying the lotion throughout the day. (Wash your hands after applying lotion so your paddle shaft won't be slippery.) Use one of the special lotions for the face, in case spray washes the lotion into your eyes.

Also good for protecting the face and head on sunny days are broad-brimmed hats, billed caps, Arab-style headdresses made from bandannas or towels, and sunglasses. Select polarized sunglasses; these not only protect your eyes from sun damage, but also allow you better glimpses of rocks beneath the water's surface. All sunglasses and prescription lenses should be strapped on, with Croakies, Chums, or other retainers (a piece of rubber surgical tubing works well, too). If you value your hat, clip or tie it on (but be careful of long straps that could entangle you). Sunglasses or goggles may be necessary to help avoid losing contact lenses should you go overboard—and carry a pair of backup glasses or lenses on any expedition.

Hats are important for cold conditions, as well. A warm knit-type cap helps retain body heat on even the chilliest days afield. Keep in mind that a lot of body heat escapes through an unprotected head. But avoid hoods that may restrict your head and neck motion—you'll need full peripheral vision on the river.

DRY BAGS AND BOXES

From whitewater suppliers, you can purchase special PVC bags that will keep your belongings dry for day trips or expeditions. Don't count on using garbage bags; these develop punctures very quickly and never last. However, heavy-duty leaf bags will work as extra protection for sleeping bags carried in IKs. Wrap the sleeping bag inside the plastic bag and secure it, then stow it in the bottom of the bigger dry bag. Zip-Loc-type baggies, especially the heavier freezer bags, provide security for socks, books, and other small items inside the larger dry bag. They also allow you to sort through your things without getting them full of sand. Small clip-on bags usually aren't totally waterproof but can carry sun lotion, Chapstick, toilet paper in a Zip-Loc bag, and other small items where they will be handy during the day.

If you will be carrying a large dry bag any distance—over a portage or up a hill to camp, for example—choose the kind with backpack-type shoulder straps for easier hauling. Your dry bag should have both a secure, foolproof closure and some means for secure tie-down (such as grommets or D-rings). For expeditions, one large bag carries more gear than several smaller bags, is easier to tie down, and is harder to lose. However, if the bag leaks, everything may get wet. Beware of cheap river bags!

A good bag, properly treated, will last for years. Always carry the bag—never drag it over sand or rocks, and never toss it down; set it down gently. Avoid using your bag as a groundsheet or porch when camping. Remember that bags can be hurt by abrasion, too, just like IKs. If you load the dry bag on a roof rack, be careful with strapping—don't let straps or the rack chafe, and secure the bag well so it doesn't fall off.

Because most dry bags are made of PVC material, they can be patched like an IK, using Vynabond or other vinyl adhesive. Carry a repair kit with a small amount of extra vinyl material to use as patches for your dry bag just in case it develops a leak or becomes torn (an air mattress patch kit works in a pinch, as will duct tape).

Waterproof boxes, barrels, and buckets, favored by rafters, are not as useful for IK paddlers. They tend to be too large to fit inside the IK, and they have hard edges that can hurt you should you fall against them. But a small Army-style ammunition can (known as an "ammo can") makes an excellent, totally waterproof camera box that is easy to operate and will safely carry expensive cameras down the river (see Photography in Chapter Eight). Small ammo cans are also good as first aid and repair kit boxes. Plastic boxes and other containers offered by whitewater equipment suppliers, such as Pelican, also keep these kits waterproofed, without as much weight.

STRAPS

Rather than tie everything down with ropes, many boaters prefer to use straps, various lengths of nylon webbing, secured by threading the loose end through a buckle. Straps are far faster and easier than tying knots and are simpler to release when unpacking. Besides securing loads, straps also attach IKs to trees when tying up for the night, or they can fasten the corners of a tarp for a quick shelter. They're handy for transporting an IK on a car roof, too. When carrying an inflated boat down to the river, or when portaging around a rapid, some paddlers rig a sling out of straps to secure the IK over one shoulder or on their backs. Straps have many uses and are sold chiefly through whitewater equipment suppliers.

You won't need webbing wider than an inch for IK duty. Choose the cam-style buckle over the quick-release buckle—it's stronger, it won't jam, and it releases almost as swiftly by depressing the cam lever with your thumb. Cams are sturdy metal buckles that will long outlast the tough nylon webbing attached to them. When the webbing finally wears out, stitch a new piece on, and the strap is ready to function once more. (For easier threading into the buckle, many boaters like to cut a triangular point into the free end of the strap. Melt the severed areas in a flame so they won't unravel.)

Fas-tex buckles of plastic make acceptable fasteners for tie-downs, although they're used more often on PFDs and dry bags than on straps. They release their grip quickly without jamming, but being plastic, are not as durable as the metal buckles. Plastic buckles are more appropriate in places where there is risk of injuring the boater (on PFDs, for example, where paddlers can hit their knuckles on the fasteners).

3

GETTING STARTED
Basic and Advanced Paddling Techniques

Before you can jump into an IK and head off on a wild river adventure, you must first master some basic skills. Your approach to learning these skills depends on your background and your personality. If you've never paddled, and you're a little nervous about being by yourself in a little boat, you may want to seek professional instruction or at least start out very slowly. If you have previous whitewater experience, enough to give you more confidence in the IK, you might be ready to start off with a bang by heading for some rapids, especially if you have paddler friends who can assist you.

The real beauty of becoming an IK user is that you are in charge of your destiny. You set the pace at which you learn to paddle, and you progress to greater challenges only when you feel ready to tackle them.

THE OUTFITTED TRIP OPTION

As the inflatable kayak option becomes more and more popular for running rivers, whitewater outfitters across the country are responding to this surge of paddle-your-own enthusiasm by offering both boats and lessons. For many people new to inflatable kayaking, paying for an outfitted river trip that features IKs makes a lot of sense. You don't have to buy an IK of your own right away—one is provided for you, usually at no additional expense. All your river equipment and meals are furnished; sometimes even camping gear is company-owned. Guides instruct you in paddling and wait below the rapids for rescues. In the evening, if you're tired from paddling, the guides are there to do the work while you rest.

On such a trip, you'll soon discover whether or not paddling an IK is your cup of tea. Although there are some negative factors associated with commercial trips, cost is not necessarily a drawback. Most commercially operated IK adventures are offered at reasonable cost (figure around $100 per day for an overnight trip, somewhat less for a day trip). Measured against the expense of a well-made IK, the cost of a fully outfitted adventure—including equipment, food, shuttle, instruction, safety backup, baggage boat, camp services, and river permits where required—is worth it, especially if you've never paddled a boat before and aren't sure you even like the idea of paddle-your-own.

The main disadvantage of commercial IK trips is that they deal in volume. It may be hard to sharpen your skills when there are two dozen other clients clamoring for attention. Often, after a brief introductory lesson, you're promptly on your own, with little additional instruction until you reach whitewater. On most trips, you won't learn real skills like how to execute an eddy turn or how to stay upright with a brace stroke. This is mainly due to the fact that few commercial IK trips operate on mild rivers, because most customers demand action. They're out for thrills, not to develop skill.

Commercial IK trips are, however, an excellent way to "test the waters," to gain access to permit-restricted rivers, and to work on your basic paddling skills and wilderness camping techniques. But, once you've decided to go this route, you face another obstacle: finding a commercial IK outfitter. Despite the growing popularity of the IK, only a handful of river outfitters offer all-inflatable kayak trips, and most of these few operate on the big western rivers. Other outfits offer you the option of paddling an IK on their raft trips— sometimes by yourself, if the whitewater is moderate enough, or most often, sharing the boat with other members of the party. (Yet another option is a hardshell kayak school. There are lots of good ones across the country and many paddle techniques are similar.)

Paddling an IK alongside a big rubber raft isn't necessarily bad, and neither is sharing the IK with others. For beginners, paddling can be exhausting, especially in a headwind. On a raft-supported trip, you can rest on the raft (towing the IK behind, or strapping it down), or you can trade off with someone else. You don't have to carry much gear—if any—in the IK, and should you strain a muscle, you can ride in the raft the rest of the way. Weigh these advantages against the fact that most rivers wide enough to accommodate large supply rafts will have lots of rafts—and lots of people. Even on a wilderness river raft trip, expect to see other parties. If you treasure solitude, perfect your IK skills on these trips, then move on to the smaller rivers and streams that are too tight for rafts. (Consult the appendix for a list of outfitters who offer inflatable kayak trips.)

TEACHING YOURSELF

Many inflatable kayakers start out on whitewater rivers, forcing themselves to learn survival paddling quickly, or else swim. Even with the most careful of guides escorting a fleet of inflatable kayaks, in most whitewater, some paddlers are sure to dump out of their boats. Because of this, IKs have acquired a reputation for being dangerous boats that are difficult to control.

But remember that paddling an IK is easy. Modern inflatable kayaks—not necessarily the cheap versions—handle very nicely on all sorts of water and teaching yourself to paddle isn't at all difficult. What takes time is building your confidence on the water and learning to "read" the rapids. Only genuine river experience—taking trip after trip—will advance you from novice to intermediate paddler.

Most anyone with average strength and coordination can become reasonably proficient in the basic IK paddle strokes after a few hours of concentrated practice. Before that inevitable first flip occurs, you should also learn what to do when ejected from the IK and practice the self-rescue technique. (With the proper safety measures you'll learn in Chapter Five, dumping out shouldn't be cause for panic.) All you need is the determination to succeed, some water to practice in, your gear—and a paddling partner. For starters, an IK, a PFD, and a paddle are all you'll need—add the rest of the gear later.

Beginning on flatwater instead of whitewater is much easier, and safer. For gaining confidence with the basic strokes, the calm inlet of a lake or a pond—even a swimming pool—is ideal. Then take your newly acquired paddling skills to a broad, slow river. You'll promptly discover that handling the IK is actually easier on moving water. The IK tracks better in a current, and, because the flow gives you a boost, paddling is less work. On a swift stream without obstacles to dodge, the IK glides along, the paddle dipped only occasionally for keeping the course straight.

POSITIONING IN THE IK

Where you sit in the IK is important for keeping the boat trim, or balanced, when afloat, and it affects how the boat handles. A common beginner's mistake is to sit too far forward or backward, which throws the IK off balance and will result in many swims if the bad habit is carried over into whitewater. Also, remember that a boat pivots (turns) around the center of the heaviest weight (you). For greatest control, the IK's pivot center should be slightly behind its measured center. (If the IK is pivoting too far toward one end or the other, it won't respond as well to your strokes, and you're likely to hit obstacles that are otherwise quite easy to miss.)

Position your weight a little back of the IK's center, which is measured from the bow's tip, about two-thirds of the way back. When you get into whitewater, you'll want the bow a bit on the light side, to ride over waves. Paddlers in Tahiti-type boats always seem to sit too far back, especially in a K-2, and then wonder why they keep spilling out of the boat.

Now, if your IK has a fixed thwart for a backrest, there isn't much leeway for balance adjustment, although you can reverse the IK and run it backwards, if the stern compartment fits you better. With a movable seat, custom balancing is possible. Be sure to fasten the seat down securely once you determine the position that's best for you.

Once at the water's edge with your IK, how do you get in? Although the IK is narrow and low to the ground, it is considerably more stable than its hardshell cousin. First, choose a shallow spot, not too rocky. Don't try to keep your feet dry. Grit your teeth and wade into the water, pushing the IK ahead of you, until it is float-

These two paddlers are leaning too far back in their IK. The improper weight distribution threw the boat off balance and flipped it over when they entered the big wave.

ing on several inches of water. Hold the paddle in one hand, steadying the IK in your other, as you slowly lower yourself, fanny-first, into the middle of the IK. It may help to have a friend hold your IK in place, at least until you're practiced in boarding.

Swing your legs into the bow, grab your paddle in both hands, settle back against the seat or thwart, and you're off. After those first few clumsy entrances, you'll soon develop a polished leap, and eventually be able to scramble in without getting your dry shoes baptized.

Your legs should lay flat on the floor, and your feet should rest almost in the tip of the bow, where both side tubes come to a point. If you're sitting too far forward (with your knees scrunched up or your feet crammed into the bow), or too far backward (more than fifteen inches or so of legroom), you'll need to adjust the IK's seating.

Remember to keep your weight *low* in the inflatable kayak. Always sit on the floor of the IK, and not on an elevated cushion, when learning to control the boat. Never sit on the thwart, on the side tubes, or on a seat that is as high as the side tubes. Carrying weight too high decreases stability and can cause the IK to overturn. In self-bailing IKs, some water may enter the boat as you sit down; the amount will depend on your weight and the make and model of your IK. The resulting puddle that collects underneath your rear end can be annoying. Some boaters need to add a thin layer—no more than an inch thick—of ethafoam or other moisture-resistant padding, in order to raise their fannies above the water line.

Experienced IKers who know how to brace are able to sit higher above the boat's water line without dumping. Some even prefer to kneel, particularly when playing with the river. And sitting on the thwart or side tube offers a relaxing break from the usual position when paddling flatwater. However, beginners should stay on the bottom, even at the risk of some discomfort, to retain the IK's steadiness. (Note that this problem with heavy boaters sitting too high in the IK is mostly a male concern. Women are naturally balanced for kayaking, carrying most of their body weight below the waist. With their greater body weight—most of it in the upper body—men may find some IK models tippy.)

THE TWO BASIC STROKES

To start paddling an inflatable kayak, all you need are the two basic strokes: the forward *power* stroke, and the reverse *backpaddle* stroke. Before discussing these strokes, however, we need to look at paddles.

The IK paddler has a choice of two types of paddles: feathered and nonfeathered. Some breakdown paddles offer both options. The flat blade surfaces (or *power faces*) of a feathered paddle are set at right angles to each other (see illustration), while on a nonfeathered paddle, they're aligned. The flat surfaces of the feathered paddle are rotated so that when one blade is stroking through the water, the other blade presents just the edge of the face to the wind, resulting in decreased wind resistance for easier paddling. Some IK paddlers begin with a nonfeathered paddle, believing it to be easier to learn, and switch to a feathered paddle as proficiency increases. Problems sometimes arise, however, when paddlers attempt to change from nonfeathered to feathered paddles, since ingrained paddling habits can be difficult to change. It is probably best to start out using feathered blades, which offer greater paddling efficiency. In addition, it may be easier to learn on a paddle with flat, rather than spooned, blades.

Begin by gripping the paddle shaft firmly with hands placed about shoulder width apart. When executing a paddle stroke, the power face of the paddle should never be horizontal to the water; try slicing a blade in this position through the water to understand the uselessness of such a stroke. Leverage to propel the inflatable kayak forward must come from the power face of the paddle being pulled through the water. When first practicing on calm water, it may be helpful to keep your eyes on each paddle face in turn as you stroke, until the proper orientation becomes automatic.

Stroking with the feathered blades takes a little coordination, and may feel awkward at first, but soon will become second nature. Choose one hand to become the master hand or *grip hand*. This is

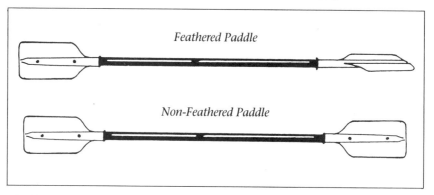

The blades, or power faces, of a paddle are set at right angles to each other on a feathered paddle.

usually the right hand, even for lefties (the following description assumes the right hand is the grip hand). The secret of stroking with feathered blades is that the paddle *never rotates* in the grip hand. Grip the paddle firmly with the right hand, with the knuckles flat, and let the paddle shaft rotate through the left hand grip. It is easiest to describe the right-hand and left-hand strokes separately.

Position the paddle to stroke with the right-hand paddle facing the water on the right side of the boat. Reach forward with the paddle, extending the right-side blade out in front of you as far forward as you can comfortably reach. Dip the blade into the water until almost completely submerged. Pull the paddle straight back alongside the boat, twisting your body to the right as your elbow reaches your hip. While you are pulling the paddle with your right arm, push the shaft forward with your left. As the blade comes alongside you, follow through with a smooth, even stroke. Lift the right blade out of the water, while at the same time raising and extending the left blade toward the left side of the bow.

For the left-hand stroke, cock the right wrist back a quarter turn, rotating the paddle shaft in your left hand, so that the power face is presented in the proper position *before* taking a stroke on the left side. Grip tightly with the left hand, and dip the left blade into the water; pull back with the left arm while pushing forward with the right arm, and lift the paddle at the end of the stroke. Then recover, snapping the right wrist down for the stroke on the right side. Again the wrist is rotated ninety degrees so that the right hand is once more in proper position. Remember that the master (right) hand grip remains fixed; the right wrist controls the motion by cocking up or backwards on the left-side stroke, then snapping down for the right-side stroke. If this sounds complicated, keep in mind that it is easier to execute than to describe in words.

When learning to work with feathered blades, paddlers may have trouble rotating the shaft so that the left blade is in proper stroking position. Improper rotation causes the left blade to slice through the water uselessly; this is why it may help initially to watch the paddle blades as you stroke. In the excitement of running rapids, sometimes even a well-practiced feathered-blade technique will falter or fail altogether. Resist the temptation to unfeather the blades—this is a step backward in your kayaking progress. Just keep working on your technique until the rotation maneuver becomes automatic.

Right, left, right, left—you're moving the IK forward. With these boats, it is necessary to keep paddling, because the boats won't track (follow a straight line) properly; paddling only on one side forces the IK to turn. That's why you must use a double-bladed paddle. It is normal for your stroke to be stronger on one side than the other, causing the boat to turn to the left or right. Over time, you will learn to compensate for this.

Don't worry too much about form at first—concentrate on smooth, easy strokes. What is important is combining left-side and right-side paddling into one smooth motion, with no hesitation between strokes. This delivers speed and power when needed. Balance is critical, too. Don't get into the habit of leaning over the sides of the boat, straining too far for a stroke. Try to keep your back pressed against the seat, stroking with your arms, shoulders, and abdominal muscles, but not with your back.

To backpaddle, simply reverse the process. Using your right hand, reach back along the side of the boat behind the seat, rotating hips and shoulders. Lower the blade to the water, again immersing the power face almost completely. Bring the paddle forward, pushing away from yourself. Repeat on the left side. Shifting sides during the backpaddle won't be quite as smooth as the forward stroke. In addition, the backpaddle stroke is less powerful. Because this is a weaker stroke, paddlers often concentrate on the forward stroke, using the backpaddle only for turns, slowing down against the current, and for the back ferry maneuver.

TURNING

Learning to change directions in any type of paddle craft is tricky, not unlike the process of learning to drive a standard transmission car. If you mull over the mechanics of turning in a critical situation, the move will come a moment too late. Practice until you can turn left or right without stopping to think which stroke to use.

For a right turn, you have two choices: either paddle forward on the left side, or backpaddle on the right side. To make a left turn, do just the opposite: paddle forward on the right side, or backpaddle on the left. Remember that to backpaddle on the *same* side as the turn is the least-complicated strategy for most paddlers. Also, a strong backpaddle stroke turns the IK immediately. For faster turns with less effort, use your paddle blade as a rudder: while your boat is moving forward, submerge the blade, then instead of pushing the paddle blade away from you, just lean hard with your weight on the paddle in the backpaddle motion. A well-executed rudder stroke comes in handy when navigating rock-strewn rivers, where quick zigzag turns are necessary and there is little room to swing the paddle.

To make the IK go where you want to go, combine two-sided forward paddling with one-sided backpaddling turns. Because a paddle-powered craft's strongest stroke is forward, get into the habit of first turning your IK toward your intended direction, then paddling forward until you get there. Whenever possible, use the forward stroke to move the IK, until you develop a strong backpaddle.

EXITING THE IK

You've just learned all you need to know for paddling in a pool, except how to make a graceful exit. Expect awkward dismounts in the beginning—balance takes time. Once more, maneuvering will be easier if you have a trusted friend to hold the IK steady. If not, try to beach the IK on a smooth surface, such as sand or a concrete boat ramp, or find something to hold onto (a branch or handy rock). Once the IK is holding still, climb on out. Don't be afraid to wade a little, but first make certain the water is shallow!

Two problems that plague novice paddlers when climbing out of IKs are deep-water dismounts (especially in waters that didn't look neck-deep), and losing their craft before they're safely beached. A moment of caution before you scramble out of the boat will prevent these embarrassments.

Should shorelines have only deep water where you must exit, seek help from someone on dry land. A person on shore can hold the IK for you and help you climb out. Avoid getting out on deep-water shores without land assistance, if you can. For unassisted landings, try a technique developed by hardshell kayakers, using your paddle as a brace. Hold it behind your seat, crosswise to the IK. Position the paddle so that one blade extends over the shore, and the other is solidly positioned behind you over the boat. Lean toward the shore onto the paddle, then hoist yourself up and out of the IK—carefully!

Now that you're safely on shore, don't forget the IK! Even without a current, wind or wake can cause an unsecured IK to float away. With a strong river current, the IK can drift out of sight in moments. When disembarking from an IK, hold onto the boat with one hand so it doesn't get away. Develop the habit of pulling the IK well out of the water, up onto the bank. Store the paddle in the IK to avoid losing it. Should strong winds threaten, tie the IK to something solid, such as a tree (IKs are light enough to blow away), and clip down your PFD as well.

OPERATING ON MOVING WATER

When confident with the basic paddle strokes, graduate to moving water. Try to pick Class I water—that is, a river with slow current, perhaps some riffles or even small waves, but no major obstacles to dodge. Eight or ten miles represents a full, hard day's paddle for beginners. You'll probably want to start out with less mileage. Go with at least one companion, for safety. And remember that rivers only go one way—you must arrange to be picked up at the end of the trip, or leave a second car at the take-out, unless you enjoy paddling against the current (and the river isn't flowing too fast for such efforts). Also, make sure you know what your take-out point looks like from the river. If in doubt, flag it with a red bandanna easily visible from the water.

Things happen much faster on a river than on flatwater. You must stay alert, even on an "easy" river. First, paddle your IK out into the middle of the river. Shorelines are often shallow and rocky, with little or no current—perfect for stalling an IK. Unless you want to stop moving, stay in the deeper, faster waters in midstream. A river current flows faster down the middle because it encounters less friction there than at the edges of the river.

By the way, in river-running terminology, right and left side of the river are your right and left side, respectively, as you face downstream. These are sometimes referred to as "river right" or "river left."

Practice forward paddling, backpaddling, turning. But practice only when the water ahead of you is clear of any obstacles. Bow first, the boat is always ready to turn and maneuver away from any approaching obstacle. On moving river water, you may encounter a midstream rock or boulder, a fallen tree, or a bridge piling. Begin your move well in advance of these obstacles. Remember to turn the IK so you are facing *away* from the obstacle, then paddle forward, *hard*.

Always give yourself extra time and distance for river maneuvers, especially as a novice paddler. When you decide to land the IK, start early. Don't wait until you are parallel with the boat ramp. Begin the move toward shore well in advance, or you might end up walking back.

One common mistake beginners often make is *broaching* (getting sideways to the current). Unless making a purposeful turn in swift waters, always keep the IK aligned with the current, especially important when floating through waves. The river current may force the IK sideways—this is an awkward position to be in, and getting sideways in a powerful current can lead to getting dumped. There may be times, however, when you need to position your boat sideways to the current—to avoid an obstacle or paddle away from a wall, for example. Make your move, then straighten out the boat as soon as possible. Use the rudder stroke to keep the IK straight.

Ferrying

Crossing a river in an IK is commonly called *ferrying*, after the ferry boats used to float people, their cars, and other belongings across moving water. The simplest kind of ferry boat uses the power of a river's current to move across the river. IK paddlers can also take advantage of this river force to move their boats across the river more easily.

Moving downstream with the current on an easy river is a cinch. But try heading upstream. Paddling immediately becomes a struggle. Yet there are times when paddling against the current, using an upstream ferry, is necessary. For instance, if you must get across to the opposite bank quickly, and the current threatens to sweep you downstream, you ferry. In an upstream ferry, your upstream paddling counteracts the downstream force of the current, while your angle to the current helps lever you across the river. Done properly, the ferry stroke turns an impossible-sounding task into a smooth glide. The secret is the angle at which you paddle upstream.

Turn the IK so that you are facing upstream at an angle to the current. Start paddling forward upstream against the current with strong strokes. You'll make progress without losing much position. Remember to paddle on both sides of the boat with this stroke, otherwise you're just turning or ruddering. You may find, however, that you need to paddle harder on one side or the other in order to maintain your diagonal orientation.

The proper angle to the current is all-important when ferrying. You must be at a sharp, diagonal angle (forty-five degrees or so, depending on the force of the current) to the current, definitely not sideways. Practice on gentle currents before attempting the ferry on fast-moving waters. Learning to anticipate the angle that will work best against a river's current takes plenty of practice.

With the *back ferry*, the principle is the same, only the operation is completely reversed. When you back ferry, you face the obstacle you want to avoid and backpaddle away from it. Again, the correct diagonal angle against the current is what makes the stroke work efficiently. Back ferrying comes in handy for clearing obstacles such as rocks without turning your back on them, and without gaining more speed towards them. When you position your IK for the traditional upstream ferry stroke—that is, when you turn upstream and paddle forward away from an obstacle—you lose sight of what lies ahead downstream. Paddlers also back ferry to maneuver in tight spots, such as when the river smashes into a cliff wall.

Experienced paddlers use the back ferry not only to avoid rocks and holes, but also to slow the IK against the current while moving laterally in the current. Slowing down gives the paddler extra time at the head of a rapid, or whenever a longer look at what the river is bringing might be helpful. Backpaddling with the bow of the IK pointed straight downstream slows the downstream momentum of the boat, while maintaining the boat's position in the current (but is not a ferry). This stroke may seem awkward at first, but soon becomes second nature.

Balance

On a moving river, you quickly learn more about balancing. The power of the current, even on a slow river, can sometimes make the biggest and widest IK feel tippy. But proper balancing counteracts this force. The same balancing techniques that work for hardshell kayakers work for IKs. Depending on your position in a strong current, one side of the IK might be sucked down, causing the opposite side to rise upward. This upward side is called the *highside*. To avoid a dunking whenever one side of the IK is forced upward, you need to counteract this force by shifting your body weight *toward* the highside. Usually, just a quick *lean* toward this highside will restore stability. Never lean away from the highside—you're sure to dump! Practice this maneuver; it will be important when negotiating whitewater.

River Reading 101

Like people, rivers have unique characteristics. The personality, so to speak, of a river can be described by its various features. All rivers share common characteristics, and you can learn to *read* a river just like reading the newspaper. With practice and study, the story hidden beneath the water's surface becomes clear. A knowledgeable boater can tell with a glance the obvious route in easier rapids, or pick a safe entry through expert-level whitewater from shore. In the next chapter, we'll learn some of the secrets that river-running experts use to read the river.

But until you're ready to tackle whitewater, avoid it. Paddle off to one side when you see the whitecaps of waves midstream. You can follow the "sneak" route, the easy side, of the rapids, until you gain control and confidence. (Be aware of the potential hazards of an extreme sneak run, though. In some rapids, the sides of the channel contain rocks, holes, and pour-overs that are not visible from above, as well as shallows, gravel bars, and turbulent eddy currents. Often the safest route is down the center channel, through those waves that only *look* intimidating.) When traveling with more knowledgeable boaters, rely on them to show the way (or the spot you will want to miss). Work on recognizing the features of rivers, because your safety on moving water will depend on your ability to distinguish rock from wave at a glance. Don't give in to the kamikaze temptation: when in doubt, sneak the route.

Rivers don't flow in a straight line—they meander, making turns, creating bends. Currents are constantly changing, readjusting to the way the river is moving. While floating, watch the way the current flows. Currents on the outside edge of a turn, for instance, are stronger, and may try to sweep the IK into the river bank or an overhanging branch. Such strong currents that are headed in a direction other than where you want the boat to go should be avoided well in advance. Get into the habit of keeping to the inside edge of the current when the river begins a sharp bend. (Don't get too close to the inside edge; rivers are likely to be shallower here, and you could become stranded on a gravel bar.)

Beginning paddlers also must learn to recognize eddies and use them effectively. Eddies are pockets of swirling water that can wreak havoc with your balance and paddling. In an eddy, the river water is actually flowing upstream, creating a strong force against the current of the river. On big-volume rivers like the Colorado, even huge rafts have been known to be trapped in these whirlpools for hours. Most eddies aren't this ferocious, fortunately, and once you know how to use them properly, they are friendly places. You can use eddies as places to stop and catch your breath, to bail, or to scout the next section of river. Practicing entering and exiting eddies in calm water is invaluable, because you may need this experience later. Learn to use eddies, not fear them.

Eddies are created by irregularities along a river, such as rocky outcroppings, midstream boulders, sharp bends, or constriction. The "eddy line" between water flowing downstream and water forced to flow upstream can upset an unwary paddler; try to avoid crossing this line until you are experienced. This is where your practice pays off.

At times, rivers also separate into distinct channels. Around an island or gravel bar, the safest route is always the route you can see the most of, preferably the channel in which you can see where the water rejoins the main current. Avoid small channels where you can't see the end; these may dead-end or run into log jams. If the end isn't visible, look to see where most of the current is flowing, and follow that channel. Also, when faced with two channels that are both blind, take the one that drops first. Experienced boaters who have made the float before know which channels to take. Follow their lead until you have sufficient experience to explore on your own.

GROUP DYNAMICS

So far, we have assumed the reader to be a solo paddler learning on calm water with a friend acting as backup. However, the easiest, fastest, and safest way to gain experience in river-running is to follow another boater who already has good experience. An experienced boater knows which rivers will suit your skill level, which routes to take through rapids, and where to wait to perform rescues, if necessary. Much of the pressure to learn whitewater skills quickly is removed when there is a good lead boat to follow. Such a lead boat doesn't necessarily have to be an IK; hardshell kayaks, canoes, and even rafts may be followed downriver successfully. Just make sure that the boater you follow is skilled—and knows your level of skill. Also, don't follow a larger boat too closely; they need more space to maneuver, and being too close to a bigger boat will cut off your view of what's coming because you sit lower in the water.

When paddling in a group, keep boats close together, for social purposes and for safety. Voices don't carry far on the river, particularly over the roar of rapids. Each boater must be able to see the boat ahead and the boat behind. The most experienced boater always takes lead (except when teaching leadership or on easy rapids) and the second-most experienced boater should always take the last position (known as the "sweep" boat). Never pass the lead boat without good reason.

By keeping the party together and descending the rapids one boat at a time, the danger of running whitewater is greatly minimized. Each boater has the responsibility of backing up the others of his or her group. The "buddy system"—everybody matched in twos—also works well: each watches the other for signs of fatigue or hypothermia.

Those two dangers—exhaustion and cold—cause more boating tragedies than either whitewater or sharp rocks. IK paddlers need to be alert and mobile, both of which are difficult when cold numbs the reflexes, or fatigue robs coordination. Situations can simmer all day—for example, a long paddle into a headwind—or suddenly erupt, such as when a paddler without adequate protective clothing gets a cold-water dunking. Groups must be prepared to handle these situations.

MENTAL GYMNASTICS

Although paddling is essentially a physical skill, accomplished with specialized equipment, the most important tool for any paddler is his or her brain. Mental preparedness is just as important as physical ability on the river. Panic, indecision, and inattention can cause accidents. This does not mean you should paddle without emotion. On the contrary, excitement and fear are good for you, causing a rush of adrenaline for quick power. Negative emotions, however, stifle your reactions. So do artificial stimulants. IK paddlers must stay in control of their mental faculties at all times, so save the intoxicants for camp . . . if you still need them after the incredible high of whitewater!

Remember rivers are always active. Stay alert—don't drift aimlessly. Pay attention to what the river is doing, and to the direction your craft is headed. You can relax on a quiet river well-known to you, but not during exploration or when running whitewater.

Paddle aggressively! Don't just sit and float into whitewater or strong currents. Take command of your IK. Paddle hard when entering big waves, unexpected reversals, and strong eddies. The IK is most stable when propelled, not just steered, through the river. Faced with an enormous wave? Power that paddle with everything you've got, and your chances of making it through will greatly improve.

Never quit paddling, thinking you won't make it. IKs are so maneuverable, often one more stroke will get you there. Many beginners give up too soon. Likewise, don't stop stroking just because you think you've made it. Underestimating the power of the river is a common mistake. Keep paddling until you're positive that obstacle is no longer a threat, until you're through the entire rapid, until you're beached on shore.

Conquering the mental side of paddling includes mastering the little things, like not letting go of the paddle until you're out of the boat. Dropping the paddle overboard is surprisingly easy, very embarrassing, and potentially dangerous . . . after all, you're up the creek without it. Also, some paddlers have a tendency to grip the paddle too hard, particularly under the strain of running rapids, causing blisters and painful wrists. Use a firm grip, but don't clutch tight. If you grip too hard, try foam paddle grips (see discussion of paddles in Chapter Two). Along the same lines, remember not to abandon an empty IK—these light craft have been known to blow away on shore, blow or drift downriver, or actually be yanked out of your hands by a strong current. Stay in control of your boat to maintain control of your fate on the river.

ADVANCED PADDLE STROKES

Once you've mastered the basic paddle strokes, you are ready to move on to the advanced techniques.

Practiced paddlers make good use of the *brace* stroke. This strong, quick employment of the paddle as a lever helps prevent upsets. To

This paddler's downstream lean helps maintain his balance in a reversal. Practice the lean and brace before you hit serious whitewater.

brace, hold the paddle straight out over the water, perpendicular to the middle of the boat, with the blade face parallel to the water's surface, slap the blade down on the surface and lean hard onto the paddle (see illustration). With a brace, you are actually using the force of the river to keep the boat right side up, and to keep yourself in the boat. The brace maintains balance, particularly in a highside maneu-

The brace stroke is used while "hole-riding" or in rapids where the IK gets knocked sideways by strong hydraulics. The paddler leans downstream and onto the paddle, pulling it toward the boat.

The paddler submerges the paddle and leans farther downstream to keep the broached IK upright.

ver. When correcting a tippy IK, always lean and brace *downstream*, not upstream. When your upstream tube highsides, leaning upstream to compensate can cause you to dump. Instead, the proper response is to lean downstream and rely on the power of the brace stroke to keep you upright. Most times, though, the highside and the downstream side will be the same. Bracing is very effective for small boats coming through powerful river currents like eddies or reversals. With thigh braces added to your boat (see customizing, Chapter Two), your brace stroke gains additional leverage, as you can lean farther away from the boat without risk of falling out.

Another advanced paddle stroke that comes in handy is the *draw* stroke. This resembles the movement for a brace stroke, except the draw can be done on either side of the IK—not just the downstream side—and instead of leaning onto the paddle, you pull the blade toward the boat. Borrowed from canoeing, the draw stroke moves the boat sideways in the direction opposite to the stroke. Draw strokes are used for turning into eddies and gaining leverage, as with bracing. To perform the draw stroke, hold one blade of the paddle straight out from the boat, the tip pointed straight down toward the water, and the flat power surface of the blade facing the boat. Submerge the blade and pull it strongly toward yourself. The draw stroke is good practice for the brace stroke you'll use in heavy water.

Kayakers also make use of the *sweep* stroke. This stroke is most useful for hardshell boats, but IK paddlers can learn to use it as well. For faster turning without losing forward momentum, use a forward sweep; for quick pivoting, a backward sweep. In a sweep stroke, you use the same basic stroking technique as a regular forward stroke, except the sweep is an exaggerated reach in a wide arc out and away from the boat. It is this extra reach that gives the stroke more power than simple, straightforward paddling or backpaddling. In an IK, sweep strokes—like brace strokes—can be made from a more secure position when foam or strap braces are installed, because of the long reaches required. In addition, the *sweeping brace*, a combination brace and sweep, offers a powerful resistance to the river's force that helps keep the IK upright.

STRENGTH TRAINING FOR PADDLING

The moderate paddling you will do as a beginner shouldn't be too stressful on your muscles, but if you plan long trips, it's a good idea to get into shape beforehand. If you will be paddling often, your muscles will adapt to the new activity, and grow stronger, but with preconditioning, you can paddle harder and longer. All paddlers, and especially casual paddlers, can benefit from a weight-training program concentrating on the upper body.

Both free weights (dumbbells in particular) and resistance machines, such as Nautilus, will strengthen the muscle groups used when paddling an IK: arms, shoulders, back, and abdominals. One great benefit of IK paddling is the toning your muscles receive while performing an enjoyable exercise. Proper paddling uses all the upper body muscles, including the abdominals, so after several trips, you body will show definite improvement—without drudgery.

GAMES FOR PADDLERS

Mastery of the paddling strokes comes from hours of practice. This isn't all drudgery. Once the basics are learned, paddlers can use fun river games to further develop their skills. Then, in addition to floating a river and running rapids, you're able to play with the moving water.

River games are an important part of paddling for the hardshell kayak clique, and for years, inflatables were snubbed as ungainly barges that could get through just about anything, but with neither grace nor finesse. However, this attitude is changing quickly with

To surf a wave or small reversal, paddle hard to reach the upstream side of the wave. Once you are in position, use the paddle to correct the IK's position in the surf, to keep it from being knocked sideways.

the advent of newer, more maneuverable IKs. With a good paddler in control, rigid IKs can perform many of the traditional hardshell kayak tricks. Before attempting these maneuvers, paddlers should know the basics of reading the river, which we'll be learning in the next chapter, and how to self-rescue (as shown in Chapter Five), because river gamers risk overturning their boats. Also, it's a good idea to have another boater wait for you below the play area, in case you dump out and have trouble self-rescuing.

Surfing a river wave is much like riding an ocean swell, except that on a river, waves are stationary, while the water moves through them. (On the ocean, the waves themselves move.) Surfing a wave involves stalling your boat on the water, and using the river's force to hitch a free ride. Basic wave surfing begins by slowing down the movement of your boat.

Look for a set of waves that are regular in shape, and evenly formed (not necessarily large, although surfing on bigger waves is easier and more exciting than on small waves). Turn your boat to face upstream as you enter the set of waves, then paddle as hard as you can, straight upstream (see illustration). This slows the movement of the boat through the waves. When the boat stalls on a wave, you're surfing. Correct with a rudder stroke to keep your boat from slipping sideways, and enjoy the ride. The back ferry can be used to surf, as well, although it is harder to stall the IK by backpaddling. Advanced paddlers *eddy out* (pull over into calm eddy water) near big waves, then paddle back upstream into the waves, or use the currents to glide across the river in an exciting version of the upstream ferry.

Small reversals, especially a long, even backcurling formation below a ledge, are fun to surf. (But stay out of nasty hydraulics that will trash you and your boat. The best way to find good surfing areas is to ask local hardshell paddlers, and accompany them on a surfing safari so you can see first-hand how it's done.) You don't want to backpaddle as you enter a hole, unless it's very small. Rather, land below the reversal and paddle upstream back into it to surf. A good, strong brace stroke is needed to keep from tipping over when "hole-riding." Also, custom-fit thigh braces help keep you in the IK while surfing reversals. If you're brave enough—and can paddle quite hard—you may discover the hardshell kayaker's "endo" (standing the boat on its bow tip). Wear your helmet for this one.

Some IK paddlers prefer to surf their boats while kneeling, rather than sitting. This position provides more power, as well as more excitement for the paddler. However, if you want to try kneeling, bear in mind that in this position, your body weight is higher, which can throw off your balance in the IK. Kneelers risk a quick exit! Yet, once you've mastered a swift and certain self-rescue, you can challenge yourself by trying different positions, and by playing with the river.

Surfing a reversal can be an unnerving experience for an unprepared paddler. The river is crashing all around you, and the IK is filling with water, even if it's a self-bailer. Keeping your cool is important—panic can tip you over. You may need to use a very strong, radical brace stroke to maintain your position in the hole, and leaning out that far requires some courage. Also, bear in mind that should you dump out of the IK, your self-bailing boat may go right on surfing without you. In addition, both you and your boat may get stuck in the churning waters for what will seem an eternity. No need for panic—the IK will wash out eventually, hopefully with you inside. Just keep bracing and leaning downstream to stay upright. Should conditions demand a quick exit from the reversal—a large raft tooling down the pike, threatening to steamroller you, for instance—then you may have to deliberately capsize the IK. Once upside-down, the IK will wash out fairly quickly. If not, abandon ship. (But, in general, never overturn your IK on purpose, or swim away from it, if you're stuck in a bad hydraulic. It's best to stay with your IK, inside it if possible, in that situation.)

Making your way in and out of river eddies is good practice for running big hairy whitewater, where your life may depend on your ability to land in a small eddy. Less dramatic, though no less essential, is the sharpening of your IK turning skills that also results from practicing eddy turns.

THE ESKIMO ROLL: NOT FOR HARDSHELLS ONLY

In some IK models, it's possible to execute a maneuver known as the *Eskimo roll*. Developed by sea-journeying Eskimo hunters, this technique rights a capsized kayak, using the paddle for leverage. During an Eskimo roll, the paddler remains in the kayak. A *spray skirt* or *spray deck* (fabric coverings for the open cockpit of the boat) will keep water out and keep the boater in the kayak. This maneuver is essential for hardshell kayaking, but is mostly theatrics for the vast majority of inflatables, because the IK's open cockpit makes rolls difficult (and unnecessary in all but the most dangerous whitewater). The width of the IK, which greatly increases its stability, also hinders Eskimo rolling. IKs more suitable for rolling are those that are narrow and decked over.

Some IKers delight in undertaking the challenge of performing the Eskimo roll. However, unless your IK is decked over, or has extensive modifications to keep you in the boat (good, solid braces), attempting an Eskimo roll will be impossible. The AIRE company claims their Lynx IK models can be rolled when equipped with their webbing braces and rigid seat, both of which help hold an experienced paddler inside (an inexperienced paddler just dumps out, rather than being held in the straps). A spray deck isn't absolutely necessary for a good roll, but some paddlers are adding Velcro-secured spray decks to their IKs anyway. Besides assisting with the roll, these also exclude cold water from the occupied part of the cockpit, increasing comfort while paddling in arctic conditions.

However, sealing off the open cockpit, which offers a fast, easy exit, can be hazardous: in whitewater, a paddler can be trapped inside a collapsed spraydeck (although with a fabric deck, you can cut yourself loose much more easily than a hardshell kayaker can). If you're interested in accomplishing the Eskimo roll, master it first in a hardshell kayak, not an inflatable. Then try the IK in a swimming pool or other very mild water before you take your unusual talent to the river. Always wear a helmet when rolling. And don't rely on the roll to replace IK self-rescue (for now, at least—as fast as IK technology and paddling skills are changing, it's possible that Eskimo-rolling IKs may soon become quite common!).

4

ANATOMY OF A RIVER

Rivers have always had an aura of mystery about them. There is something about their constant motion, unaided by any power source other than simple gravity, that rivets the viewer's eye; indeed, on occasions a river appears almost like a hypnotic force that holds you in its spell as you stare, transfixed by the magic of moving waters. To understand the science behind the mystery of the current is not to lose your sense of wonder; rather, knowing how a river operates increases your appreciation.

For the novice boater, "reading" a river seems an esoteric talent, a complex skill on the level of learning Latin, perhaps. And then there are those who consider getting through a rapid more a matter of luck than skill, who don't realize that learning how and where to put your boat in whitewater is no more difficult than—and not nearly as hazardous as—mastering driving in heavy traffic.

Much can be learned about how a river works by simple observation. Spend an afternoon studying how moving water is affected by the obstacles it encounters. Look upstream at a rapid and notice where rocks are located. Then walk up to the head of the rapid and look downstream to see how the rocks appear from a river runner's point of view. Even a small creek is governed by the rules of hydrology, and into such small water you can throw sticks to see how they "run the rapids." If you have a rapid regularly run by boaters close at hand, you're in luck. Spend a Saturday watching other boats run the rapid. Where did successful boaters position their craft, and what did unsuccessful boaters do wrong?

Every river is different, yet also alike. Even the tiniest creek follows the rules of moving water when it encounters an obstacle. Rivers vary according to their volume (how much water), gradient (how steep the slope), and velocity (how fast the water is moving).

They are often categorized by the pattern of their flow. A river that has rapids alternating with long quiet stretches is known as a *pool-and-drop* river and is a different river to run than one that drops steadily over its length. Pool-and-drop rivers are much easier, on the average, for boating, because there is plenty of room for recovery below each rapid. Also, running constant whitewater is demanding. Even if a fast-moving river has no big rapids, it can be tougher to paddle than one with both fast water and quiet reaches. But, if the current is smooth and constant, an IK can coast along, freed of the paddling required to traverse quiet pools.

TYPES OF RIVERS

Rivers may also be evaluated by the type of whitewater present. A river with lots of volume that creates giant rapids may be characterized as *big* water. Boaters may expect to encounter heavy hydraulics—strong river currents—on such a river, but often only basic skills are required for getting through the rapids, because big water tends to be straightforward (lacking the twists and turns and obstacles that make maneuvering difficult). On the other hand, a river described as *technical* has many tight passages, requiring practiced paddling skills to negotiate. Many rivers begin as big water in early spring, when snowpacks are melting and rain is falling, then become increasingly technical their flows decrease, exposing more rocks.

A prime example of serious whitewater for an IK. This is Class V: very steep, with narrow passages and difficult rescue. Definitely helmet water! This is Mushroom Rapid on California's Cherry Creek, which drops 200 feet per mile. Photo of Jeff Bennett by Mike Doyle.

RATING THE RAPIDS

In the whitewater community, both rivers and individual rapids are rated according to their degree of difficulty. When perusing guidebooks, you'll often encounter the International Scale of Whitewater Difficulty, which is used worldwide. With this system, whitewater runs are rated on a scale of Class I through Class VI, with Class I being easy water and Class VI virtually unrunnable. Traditionally, the Class VI rating has been reserved for rapids that have never been run successfully. With modern advances in equipment, and higher skill levels, boaters are redefining the limits of runnable whitewater. Although expert IK paddlers have successfully run some very hairy Class V water, IKs don't belong on true Class VI rapids. The argument over whether a certain waterfall is a Class VI or a Class U (unrunnable) rapid matters little to IK paddlers—plan on portaging.

Another scale, known as the Western scale, is less commonly used, appearing mostly on maps of some Western rivers. For example, rapids in the Grand Canyon are rated on a scale of 1 to 10 (easiest to most difficult). Some boaters prefer the Western scale because it is more precise. However, since most river information uses the International Scale exclusively, you should definitely become familiar with that scale—and with your individual skill level.

Paddlers, also, can be rated according to their abilities to handle difficult whitewater. Matching the degree of river difficulty to your skill level is crucial for a safe, enjoyable trip. Trying to boat water beyond your skills is more than just dangerous. Especially for nervous novices, being out of control in a rapid or dumping unexpectedly, or both, can be traumatic. Many new paddlers, particularly spouses of experienced paddlers, have been scared away from running rivers because of a rude introduction to the sport. It's best to start slowly and work your way up to the tougher stuff.

Respect the river. Even an easy rapid demands attention: IKs can flip in Class II rapids, or even on unrated water when, for instance, one is paddling against a strong eddy fence. A rapid might be rated Class II because there is a clear route past a tricky reversal, so the rating system assumes boaters will take this easy path. But if you paddle into the reversal, you're into a Class III situation. Keep in mind that rapids may be over- or underrated, depending on who rated them. Experts tend to gloss over minor rapids that may be challenging for an IK paddler (and experts in big rafts or tough hardshells are the ones who usually write the guidebooks). On the other hand, beginners tend to exaggerate the difficulties encountered.

Rapids change as well, especially with higher-than-normal water levels. A straightforward Class III in medium water levels could easily be transformed into a Class V nightmare should the river rise overnight. A dangerous strainer (a downed tree that allows current to flow through but may trap a boat or swimmer) washed into an easy rapid will elevate the skill level needed to negotiate the run—at least until the tree works loose. Other factors that increase the degree of difficulty also should be taken into consideration when investigating a run. A remote waterway automatically requires a higher level of skill than one that parallels a highway, simply because help is readily available near civilization. Rivers flowing through steep gorges offer spectacular runs, yet require caution, as you might not be able to walk out after losing a boat. Cold water creates an additional hazard for boaters. A river known for harboring many sharp rocks or lots of strainers is tougher than a similar river without such obstacles. Rapids without "clean" runouts are more difficult than those followed by long, quiet pools where swimmers can easily self-rescue. Rapids that come one right after another are harder than those with calm stretches between—even continuous Class II can be tiring (though exhilarating). Also consider your equipment—a vinyl IK has no business bouncing around in a Class IV rapid scattered with razor-edged rocks.

Besides ranking individual rapids, the International Scale also rates specific stretches of rivers according to their overall degree of difficulty. A river with Class II and Class III rapids will usually be rated as Class III; Class III skills are required to safely negotiate this river. To be more precise, some use a plus or minus sign with the classification. For example, Class II+ is more difficult than Class II, yet easier than Class III; Class III– is harder than Class II+, easier than Class III. A section of river might be rated Class III (IV), which means mostly Class III rapids with a few (one or perhaps two) Class IV drops. If the Class IVs are portaged (carried around) or lined (led along the bank by rope, like a dog on a leash), a person with Class III skills can handle the river. If there are several tougher rapids, the entire run may be listed as Class III-IV, and you may expect two or more Class IV rapids.

When researching a river, keep in mind that guidebooks usually cover a specific section of the river, or "run"—that is, from one launch area to a take-out. For example, don't confuse the lower Klamath River, a Class III (IV) run, with the upper Klamath, a Class IV-V run.

THE INTERNATIONAL SCALE OF WHITEWATER DIFFICULTY

CLASS 0—Flat water.

CLASS I—Very Easy. Waves small; passages clear; obstacles (such as sandbanks or bridge piers) easy to spot well in advance and avoid.

CLASS II—Easy. Rapids of moderate difficulty; passages mostly clear, some maneuvering required.

CLASS III—Medium. Waves numerous, high, and irregular. Rocks and eddies present. Rapids with clear passages, but may be through narrow spots, requiring expertise in maneuvering. Scouting may be necessary.

CLASS IV—Difficult. Long rapids; waves powerful and irregular. Dangerous rocks and boiling eddies. Passages difficult to scout; powerful and precise maneuvering required. Scouting mandatory first time. Risk of overturning or wrapping boat, and long swims for paddlers. For very skilled boaters.

CLASS V—Very Difficult. Extremely difficult, long, and very violent rapids, following each other almost without interruption; river bed extremely obstructed. Big drops; violent current; very steep gradient. Scouting mandatory but often difficult. Risk of boat damage and serious injury to paddlers. For teams of experts with excellent equipment.

CLASS VI—Extraordinarily difficult. Difficulties of Class V carried to extremes of navigability. Nearly impossible and very dangerous. For teams of experts only, at favorable water levels and after close study with all precautions.

CLASS U—Unrunnable. Niagara Falls or equivalent. Foolish to attempt!

(Chart based on American Whitewater Association River Classification System.)

VOLUME AND FLOW

Probably the most obvious difference among rivers is volume, the amount of water flowing past a certain point along the river's length. This is most often expressed in terms of cubic feet per second, or cfs for short. Knowing a river's average cfs gives you some idea how broad the river will be—lots of water takes up room. Volume also influences the river's speed and, to a certain degree, the size and ferocity of whitewater (keep in mind that the mighty Mississippi isn't known for its exciting whitewater).

Boaters plan their entire season around the varying volumes of rivers. Typically, rivers are controlled by three factors: dam releases, snowmelt, and rain. Dam-controlled rivers often offer some of the most reliable flows, yet also arouse the ire of many river-runners, because many miles of excellent whitewater often lie buried behind these concrete barriers. To add insult to injury, authorities in charge of water releases at the dams almost never take into consideration the needs of whitewater boaters. Dams are built for flood control, crop irrigation, and generating electric power. Although dam builders sometimes claim "increased recreational opportunities" as a justification for a new dam, this usually means a new reservoir to waterski on, not better control of water releases for whitewater boating below the dam. Advantages offered by dam control are steady water flow throughout the season (on most rivers) and a ready source of information about water levels.

Then there are the true wild rivers controlled only by nature. These are fed by springs, melting winter snows, or by torrential spring rains. Of the three, rivers fed by springs are much more dependable, because water continues to bubble up from underground at a constant, steady flow, except in extreme drought conditions. Second in reliability are rivers fed by snowpack, because the snow occurs before the float season and can therefore be measured in advance. There's always a chance that heavy snows can melt off early, should the weather turn unseasonably warm, but in general a heavier snowpack means a longer and more enjoyable float season for the rivers in its drainage. Rivers that require lots of rain to bring them up to a floatable level are most unpredictable. Boaters who hope to get on such rivers need flexible schedules, so they can take off on a trip whenever the rains arrive. This criteria is changing, however, as IK paddlers challenge the "lower limits" of boating, often running rivers below the minimums recommended in the official guidebooks.

GRADIENT

A river's gradient, or slope, is determined by the steepness of the riverbed, usually expressed in terms of drop per mile. Rivers run from higher to lower elevations, and it's this drop in elevation that creates a river's speed. A slow river will drop ten feet per mile or less. In general, the higher the gradient, the more technically difficult the rapids. A gradient of twenty feet to the mile offers good current without too much force—many moderate rivers drop at this rate. Rivers that drop fifty to one hundred feet per mile are very swift and difficult to navigate. Sharp turns, narrow passages, steep drops, few eddies to stop in, and fast water pouring into obstacles all contribute to the difficulty of a high-gradient river. Remember also that drop per mile is *averaged* over the length of a river—that twenty-foot drop per mile could be a steady current, easy to paddle, or it could be one high waterfall. The drop of the Colorado River in the Grand Canyon averages less than eight feet per mile, and this "slow" river contains some of the largest rapids on the continent.

RAPID RAPIDS

Whitewater is created by elevation loss, which is why a rapid is often referred to as a "drop." A river's drop causes the exhilarating speed of its rapids. The combination of current and impediments, such as bends in the river, boulders, or cliff walls, forms whitewater features such as eddies, waves, and reversals.

The drop of a rapid is a major reason for *scouting*, or walking along the shore to look at a rapid before you make the run. Most big rapids are also steep and drop quickly out of sight. Because of the paddler's low position in the IK, big rapids will be difficult to see far enough in advance to plan a route. Thus, the need for scouting.

IT'S THE WATER

Rivers also vary according to water temperature, color, clarity, and even texture. Cold, clear, blue waters are found in many mountain streams, while desert rivers like the Colorado are usually reddish-brown and full of silt. Expect colder water temperatures in most dam-controlled rivers, because water to be released is usually drawn from the bottom of the reservoir, where it's coldest. (Warmer water near the reservoir surface is seldom poured over the dam.) Warm waters, when you can find them, offer delightful paddling. When paddling a tropical bay isn't convenient, try rivers that are winding through valleys, rather than crashing down mountain slopes—this extra meandering allows the waters to be warmed by the sun. Also, many rivers warm up when water levels drop in mid or late summer. Just don't expect warm rivers to be clear and beautiful; the temperate waters usually promote the growth of heavy, view-obscuring algae.

Silt—from glaciers or mudslides—suspended in the current is a natural condition on some streams, or may be induced (by heavy rains, for example) on others. Grit washed downstream from glaciers is so thick on some Alaska rivers that few fish other than the specially adapted grayling can survive; at times you can actually hear the silt rustling like sandpaper over the river rocks. Silty waters obscure obstacles, making the river harder to read. On a clear stream, rocks and shallows are far more obvious.

ROCK RECOGNITION

Learning to recognize river rocks from a distance will save much wear and tear on your nerves, and your IK. While hitting rocks isn't usually serious, just ramming a small rock unexpectedly can throw you out of an IK. The IK can become pinned against a rock that has strong current crashing into it. Every rock your IK hits does a little bit of damage, too, and it all adds up.

Although huge boulders jutting far above the surface are obvious, smaller rocks tend to be sneakier. Hidden rocks just below the surface are sometimes called "sleepers"—for good reason. When looking for rocks in moving water, watch for the characteristics that signal them. Water piles up on the upstream side of a rock, creating a hump (known as a *pillow* or *cushion*) which may or may not cover the rock entirely. Once you recognize rock humps, you can position yourself to avoid most of a river's rocks. Also look for spray shooting up above or behind a rock. Water pouring over a drop, striking a rock, and shooting upwards often creates a roostertail effect—keep an eye out for these.

A series of waves tends to be regular in configuration, and rocks below the surface will upset the pattern. If the last wave in a series of waves doesn't fit in, a rock may be lurking underneath. Look closely into the white froth for a glimpse of darkness that signals rock.

A paddler enters innocent-looking Class III rapid. Note that the whitewater in front of the IK appears to be a large, fun wave.

A careful scout from a high vantage point on shore, combined with close study, reveals a nasty hidden boulder under the "wave." Study tougher rapids thoroughly, looking for a flash of darkness through the white foam that signals "rock." Now the route is obvious—head for river left or far right to avoid the boulder just right of center.

Another rock indicator is sound. Water flowing over a rock near the surface sounds different—to the whitewater-trained ear—from uninterrupted current. In a big rapid, with water crashing all around you, this isn't very useful, but learning to listen to what the river has to say can warn you of upcoming sleepers.

REVERSALS

Water flowing downhill over a rock curls back upstream, creating a pocket of boiling water, known as a *reversal,* below the hump. (Because this phenomenon resembles a hole in the river, reversals are often called "holes" by river-runners. Large, nasty reversals may be referred to as "hydraulics.") These upstream currents are often quite strong, especially in large reversals or those where much of the river is diverted over a rock or other obstacle (such as a concrete dam). Paddlers need to be able to recognize and avoid reversals, because the powerful currents can easily overturn IKs.

Navigating a rapid isn't difficult if you scout carefully and find a good route, then stick to it. Close scrutiny reveals a small tongue, hard to see, on the left side of the big reversal—offering a good route for these conservative paddlers.

From upstream, rocks with reversals behind them generally look different from waves. Watch for what looks like a letter "V" pointing *upstream*—a rock at the pointed tip of the V is creating an obstruction in the current. A spot of calm water amid flowing currents indicates an eddy or reversal behind a rock—avoid it unless you know for sure what you're looking at. Water humping over a rock and forming a reversal can also be indicated by a horizontal line that appears as you look into a rapid. Sometimes you can tell a reversal from a wave from upstream by watching how the spray breaks. Because reversals are created by an abrupt drop over an obstacle, they are often difficult to discern at a distance. The best way to see them is scouting from shore.

AVOIDING ROCKS

Start your move to avoid upcoming rocks well in advance, even if you're not sure that what you see is a rock. The cautious approach will cause you to miss some fun waves and minor holes, but they'll still be there next time, when you're more experienced.

Remember that if you are about to broach a rock, and can't avoid the collision, lean towards the rock. If you follow instinct and cringe back from the rock, you may fall out of the IK, or the IK could become pinned against the rock by strong currents. Many river rocks have a "padding" on the upstream side, created by the pillow, that keeps boats and swimmers from crashing—but don't count on this to keep you out of trouble.

Especially on the outside bend of a river, currents tend to sweep you into cliff walls or big boulders. You need to anticipate this well in advance and begin correcting course immediately. Rather than turn and paddle away, try the back ferry—that is, paddle backwards, away from the cliff or boulder.

On some rivers, especially those termed technical, there will be rapids strewn with rocks and boulders. Called "boulder gardens" or "rock gardens" depending on the size of the rocks in question, these rapids offer either a fun slalom course or a descent into pinball terror, depending on the degree of difficulty and your experience in avoiding rocks. Scout these rapids so you can plan a careful route. Use the eddies that form behind the rocks to assist your turns or slow your IK down, if the *eddy fences* (dividing lines between upstream and downstream current) aren't too strong. If you end up swimming, stay upstream of your IK until you're past the boulders.

WAVES: RIVER ROLLERCOASTERS

Waves, for the most part, are friendly features. The thrill of riding high-cresting river waves is what lures many boaters—especially IK paddlers—to whitewater. River waves differ from ocean waves in that they're stationary, often called *standing waves*. The waves actu-

Running standing waves. Keep the bow headed straight, and paddle hard through troughs and into crests.

ally stand still, while the river's current runs through them, so they always look the same, unless the water levels change. Ocean waves, however, move with the tide, so they are always changing. The dip between a series of waves is known as the *trough*—a good place to take a quick breath of air if you're swimming through.

A wave train is an easily-recognizable river feature caused by the release of a river's energy at the base of a drop. Waves may be smooth and regular in shape, offering good rides and surfing opportunities, or irregular, such as a *backcurler*, a wave with a punch that may overturn an unwary boater. (A backcurler is similar to a reversal.) Very large waves are occasionally referred to as *haystacks*, because the huge mounds of water do somewhat resemble piles of hay.

If you know for certain the waves are clean—devoid of hidden rocks or reversals—then go for them! Run waves by lining up the IK with the center of the first wave, then paddle hard into it, and keep paddling until you're up and over the crest. Continue paddling forward into the wave train, hard and fast if the waves loom large over you, so you won't stall out. On the other hand, if you want to try surfing, the general idea is to deliberately stall out in the waves for a free ride.

Should the IK get tossed sideways by a big wave—common in heavy water—straighten out before the next wave. If you can't, lean downstream and brace hard and hope for the best. Just because huge waves often overturn IKs is no reason to avoid them. That's part of the challenge! But before you run big waves, know what lurks below them; if the runout isn't clean it's best to "sneak" the waves, taking the easier route to avoid a flip.

RIVER LUMBER

Especially during spring floods, rivers can carry a lot of debris: fallen trees, overhanging branches, sticks wedged between rocks. River runners have their own pet names for such timber, such as "strainers" (downed trees that allow the current to pour through them, but strain anything else, like boats, into their branches), or "alligators" (protruding sticks or logs, which resemble the big reptiles lurking beneath the surface, with just the nose visible—capable of taking a bite out of your boat).

The danger of trees lodged into the river's current is twofold. First, the strong force of moving water plowing into the obstacle can create a suction that may pin or overturn an IK, or even suck both boat and paddler under. A paddler will usually flush through, but could be caught underneath the strainer and drown. Second, strainers can appear overnight after a flood, windstorm, or land-clearing operations, surprising unwary boaters.

Don't go anywhere near downed or overhanging trees, especially if the current near them is strong, which it usually is. Move to avoid them well in advance, with lots of clearance. Also keep alert for logs pinned against rocks; you should be able to see a disturbance in the water, and make out the form of the log just under the surface (well-buried logs are no threat). Another nasty wood hazard is a log jam, which you may encounter unexpectedly at the bottom of a blind drop or around a tight bend of the river. If you see logs ahead, back-paddle like mad, or turn away from the obstacle and paddle forward to make sure you miss it. Particularly in early spring, when logs are washing down the rivers, keep alert for stray timber.

CHOOSING A ROUTE

In whitewater, look for the path of least resistance. A route that bypasses obstacles, or offers an easy paddle around them, is always better than one that takes you to the brink of disaster. Until you are a very skilled paddler, look for the easy way.

Many rapids offer an obvious, easy channel known to river runners as the *slick* or *tongue*, sometimes as a *chute*. A tongue is shaped like a *downstream* "V" (Vs pointing upstream indicate rocks and/or reversals). In a simple, straightforward drop, a broad tongue leads into a series of standing waves. Positioning your IK at the middle of a tongue is almost always the best route. The smooth water offered by the tongue provides a few extra seconds to prepare for upcoming whitewater. But, because there may be a rare instance when a "rogue" tongue leads directly into disaster, you should always scout an unknown rapid, even if there is a very obvious tongue to follow, unless you can see all of the rapid.

The Importance of Scouting

To scout a river is to beach your IK and walk downstream to get a preview of what an upcoming rapid looks like before you try to make your run. Scouting is necessary to run many rapids safely, especially in an IK, because of the characteristic drop of a river as it plunges through major rapids. Not only does the river drop out of sight, but IK paddlers sit low in their boats, so they can't see the details of an upcoming rapid far enough in advance to maneuver properly. A nasty hole in the middle of a steep rapid may appear to be a great wave when viewed from the seat of an IK—double-check from shore before you get trashed. Getting a sneak preview of what's ahead makes IK boating much safer and more enjoyable; not only can you see what obstacles to avoid, you can also identify fun rollercoasters you don't want to miss. Having a good lead boat to follow can cut down on the need to scout smaller rapids, but there's nothing like an overview of a rapid beforehand to ensure a good, clean run.

Always scout any place on a river where you can't see what is coming. Blind corners above hairy rapids are not uncommon, and it takes only a few moments to get out and look. Besides, it's a good opportunity to stretch your legs. While floating, keep alert for landmarks that signal major rapids (often identified in guidebooks), as well as warning signs that usually indicate big drops ahead: noise, spray, an abrupt change or drop in the horizon line, a wall of boulders across the river. You may also anticipate encountering rapids when a river enters a narrow gorge. Beware of blind drops—don't run anything you can't see clearly—and look out for easier rapids that lead into nasty drops.

When you scout a rapid, look for obvious obstacles and routes around them. Then look for obstacles that are not as obvious, especially in rapids with high ratings. You will want to walk the entire rapid from shore if it's a big one you're not familiar with, or if the route isn't clear. From downstream looking up, it's much easier to spot hidden rocks and reversals. Also check the end of the rapid to see where you will be when you finish up, and to make sure there aren't more rapids waiting below.

In addition to spotting obstacles, you'll need to look for recognizeable features to serve as mental reminders when you make the run. Identifying landmarks in a rapid is important because of the IK's low visibility. From a high vantage point during a scout, the correct path seems quite obvious; but when you settle down into the IK's low cockpit and start into the rapid, you'll find yourself paddling into a confusing maze of foam and rocks, because the river drops below your line of vision so quickly. A landmark can be any feature easily recognizable from the water, such as a rock in the river or along the shore (preferably one with a unique, memorable shape so you'll recognize it easily), a tree, or a cliff wall. A prime example is "Volkswagon Rock" midway through Blossom Bar Rapid on the Rogue River. But most landmarks you'll be using are likely to be less obvious objects.

For instance, suppose that to avoid hidden obstacles halfway through the rapid, you've determined you should line up with a small tongue approximately right of center. The tongue will be hard to locate, because it's small. But then you notice a flat-topped rock at the top of the rapid to the right of the tongue; there's a tuft of bright green grass or a small tree growing on it. Tell yourself, "Line up to the flat rock with the greenery on it, then go three feet to the left of the rock." You may also make use of an artificial landmark, such as a brightly clad person who stands near the spot you want to be, or even a red flag hung in the appropriate place.

Remembering to divide the river into sections as you scan the rapid from shore helps, too. It's much easier to find a slot that is "about five feet left of center" than one that is "somewhere on the left side of the river." Also keep in mind that the rapid's features will be much larger when you paddle through than they look from high above. Walk down to the river's edge, if possible, to get a better perspective of how big those waves really are—before you convince yourself the rapid is easy.

If there is any chance at all of slipping and falling into the river while scouting, wear your PFD while you trek out for a look. Most boaters do, anyway, out of habit, and it's a good habit to get into.

After you've looked over the entire rapid and decided on a course, pause at the top of the rapid on the way back to your IK. A second look at the entry is always a good idea, and it's important to do this last, so that the all-important entry position is the foremost thought in your brain. How you enter a rapid determines how the whole run will go; a proper entry into a major rapid greatly increases your chances of a successful run. If the entry slot is hard to find, taking a final look from the water's edge is worthwhile, so you can see what the entry will look like from the IK.

If other boaters are coming through the rapid, it's educational to watch them from your scouting position, even if they aren't paddling IKs. Having a visual image of the proper route helps. Someone in your party may elect to run first, so that others can watch. In any case, you want to be sure you don't emulate a bad run. Watching another boat run first is especially important in rapids where following another boat is difficult or impossible (such as through a tight bend in the river or a boulder garden where the lead boat disappears from sight quickly).

The time required for scouting depends on your experience and the difficulty of the particular rapid. Some boaters get by with just a quick look, others may take over an hour to investigate a tough drop. Depending on the configurations of the river, scouting from both shores may be necessary. Some boaters considering a course like to toss sticks into the river, to better judge where a certain current will take their boats. You need to spend enough time to become comfortable with your route and to see all of the rapid that requires scouting (if it tapers off in a set of standing waves, for example, it's usually safe to assume you don't need to look at the waves).

However, it's best not to spend too much time scouting. Looking at whitewater builds up adrenalin, which your body needs to release. Delaying the release of this pent-up tension for too long can make you jumpy, and paddling will be harder if you're shaky.

With an experienced leader, scouting is easier. The experienced person can point out routes and rescue points, and even draw diagrams in dirt or sand to make sure the route is clearly understood by all. When indicating a certain rock or other river feature, everyone needs to be talking about the same thing. If there is any confusion, use diagrams, or indicate the feature in question by tossing a stone or stick onto it.

When choosing a route from shore, you have the leisure of changing your mind. On the water, you usually won't have that luxury, but have an optional route in mind, anyway, should something go wrong with your first choice. Generally, it's best to take the easiest, least-complicated, safest-looking route, unless you want to test your skills, in which case, be sure that if you don't make the alternate route, you won't be in trouble.

STARTING OFF STRONG

Concentrate on making a proper entry into the rapid, because that sets the tone for the rest of the run. A sloppy entry usually means a sloppy run. If the approach is slow, backpaddle into it, so you can take a few extra seconds for a last look at where you're going. Some IK boaters in very stable models like to stand up, or get up on their knees, for a better look, but if you do, be careful not to tumble overboard. Once you've decided on the route, don't change your mind midstream unless there is a good reason, such as another boater in trouble ahead of you.

As you start off from shore into a big rapid, it's natural to feel nervous. Take some deep breaths to help you relax. Visualize your boat in the proper route. Tell yourself you can make it. Also offer encouragement to other boaters, especially if they seem uncertain. (But don't force someone who is terrified, or facing whitewater beyond their ability. If someone is just too scared to paddle safely, have them carry around or let another paddler take their boat. There's always next time. Don't be a whitewater bully, browbeating timid paddlers into running rapids beyond their ability.)

Paddlers need to maintain enough distance between boats so that no one is crowded or cut off from their route, yet stay close enough to see what others are doing and render aid if necessary. Begin with smooth, strong strokes. Line up for a clean entry, make perfect pivots around those obstacles, keep paddling hard through big waves, and yell if you feel like it!

KNOWING A RIVER

The more times you run a river, the better you will know the river. There are four different ways to know a river: your personal knowledge based on previous experience with the river, someone else's knowledge of the river (from a companion or a guidebook writer), reading the river, and comparing the river to others you already know.

Experience is the best teacher when learning to read rivers. Every trip adds to your ability, even an easy trip on flat water. Seeing different rivers sharpens your river-reading skills, because on a new river, you're not relying on a memory of this particular river, you're starting from scratch. When you are forced to read a new river as you go, your interpretive skills improve. Even the next trip down a familiar river will seem easier.

To continue the learning process, keep challenging your skills. Run different rivers, at different water levels. Don't just float down a river—ferry back and forth across, surf waves and small holes (bigger ones, if you're brave), land in every eddy. The more you do, the more you can do.

Whether you wish to progress into expert-class whitewater (Class IV-V) or stay at the intermediate level, where it's safer, is up to you. It's possible to have lots of fun, excitement, and challenge on Class III rivers, especially if you play on them all the way down. Plunging through giant waves and holes isn't for every paddler, so don't feel pressured to keep increasing the difficulty level of the rivers you float. Your skills will continue to improve even on moderate rivers.

How To Run Low Water

IK paddlers dance to a different tune, especially in drought-stricken areas of the West. They're doing the "river limbo": how low on the flow can you go? Rather than put their boats on the shelves during a dry spell, IK paddlers are discovering the joys of navigating low water. Besides extending the boating season, low-water paddling offers greater opportunities for solitude and isolation, because bigger boats can't or won't attempt such runs.

Also, the river is less pushy at lower water levels. Yes, there are more obstacles to avoid, but the river is moving more slowly, allowing extra time for viewing rapids and making decisions. Less volume means reduced power, as well, so the river may be more forgiving—a nasty "wrap-rock" at regular flows may become a "nudger" in diminished flows.

Low water doesn't necessarily guarantee an easy trip, though. Some rapids that are easy to run at normal levels will have to be lined or portaged because there won't be enough water to maneuver at lower levels. Constant rock-dodging is exciting, yet can be tiring. Also, just because an IK can fit down many rivers at low water doesn't mean every river will be runnable; getting stuck is a risk on a river no one has floated at a low level before, and you could be forced to walk out if the river proves too tough. Choosing a pool-and-drop river allows time to rest between rapids and guarantees at least some water for paddling, even if many rapids prove unrunnable. Even at extremely reduced flows, pools tend to remain deep and long. Also, a river with well-defined channels offers better low-water paddling than one that scatterguns its flow through rapids, because routes will be easier to find and navigate.

For most low-water runs, you'll need a strong, well-built IK to handle the inevitable collisions with rocks and the occasional scraping along the river bottom in shallow waters. Foam-floored IKs perform very well in low-water conditions; the foam glides smoothly over rock surfaces without getting hung up, and you never have to worry about puncturing the floor. Self-bailers are a big help, also, because surplus water in the bottom of the IK adds drag. A short, narrow IK fits better into tight slots and turns more quickly than a broader, longer IK. Load the IK light so it will be more maneuverable and easier to float over shallows.

Grounding out—getting stuck on the bottom of the river—is part of the limbo game. To avoid the frustration of grinding to a halt in every shallow spot, keep looking ahead for signs of shoals. If the river is clear, the color change alone should alert you to shallows: watch for the blue/green of the river changing to various shades of brown. In murkier waters, watch the surface of the river; follow waves, and go where most of the water is going. River current favors the high bank, and the outside of bends. A good paddler with strong river-reading skills can avoid most shallows. If unavoidable shallows loom ahead, aim for the deepest part and paddle hard. You want to work up some momentum to clear the shallows. Slowing down only means you'll get stuck sooner.

Eddies behind rocks offer deeper water for an IK, and a detour route past tight or shallow spots. Land in the eddy and work your way across the river—upstream, using the eddy's calm waters—until you're past the obstacles. This works well in tight rock gardens.

IKs have a shallow draft, and depending on how much weight you're carrying, they'll still float in just inches of water. If you get stranded in shallows, removing your body weight from the IK usually frees the boat. Push the IK, walking carefully alongside, until you reach deeper water, then climb back in and resume paddling. The IK can be walked through minor rapids in this fashion, as well. But don't try this in swift current, because you could get knocked down and hurt—never stand in fast water (see Chapter Five).

Likewise, don't automatically jump out of the boat if you're stuck on a midstream rock, where the current is likely to be stronger than in the shallows. Try to push yourself free first, using hands or paddle (but be careful not to break either). Wiggle your rump around—this shifts your weight. Dip your paddle into the fast-moving water, using it as a lever. Have a buddy throw you a rope from shore and pull you loose. Or perhaps another IK coming from behind will deliver a friendly bump that jolts your IK loose. If all else fails, slip out of the boat carefully, lowering just your legs off the IK's tubes, and try to push off with your feet. Climbing out of the boat to push it off a rock is your last resort.

Before you run low water, hone your rock-reading skills. Even the toughest boat will, eventually, be damaged by constant collisions with rocks. Most rocks can be avoided; don't crash into them just to prove how strong your IK is. Occasionally, you'll have a choice between hitting a small, smooth rock or ramming a big, jagged rock—choose the lesser of two evils! When forced to tow your IK, lift it, don't drag it, over rocks.

Handling Big Whitewater

Big rapids demand vigilance, and strong, skilled paddling. Don't attempt large-volume rivers until you're ready for them. The main problem with lots of water flowing past you is the incredible force of the current. This force is extremely deceptive—you don't realize how powerful the river is until you start fighting it. On a strong river, even a skilled swimmer will have difficulty crossing the current. Controlling a paddle is harder, and obstacles are more difficult to avoid, because the swift current is forcing you into them at greater speed than on flatwater.

You'll need to scout big-water rapids very carefully, always from shore, because you just won't see the trouble spots when you are sitting down low in an IK. Always have a backup waiting below each major rapid when you run big water. This is no place for solo IKs! Expect to swim a lot. If the water's at all cold—and most big-water rivers are—wear protective clothing.

The IK's light weight and small size, a blessing on tight technical waters, put it at greater risk of being *trashed* (tossed around and flipped over) in big water. If you choose to run big water, that's a risk you must assume. Be ready with a solid self-rescue.

Waves can be huge, and your IK will want to surf them all, even if you don't want to. Counter this force by paddling hard into the big waves, so the IK doesn't slide backwards. Because the IK is small, it must climb over big waves. Stop paddling, and the IK falters. If you get knocked sideways by a powerful wave, correct immediately so the IK doesn't flip. Waves with a strong back-curl effect may be hard to punch through. For these, be sure to line up straight well in advance, if possible. Then paddle hard on your approach, to build up your speed, and don't stop paddling as you hit the back curl.

Keep a lookout for eddies, especially when scouting big rapids. These offer a safe landing place, a temporary haven from the heavy rapids around you. If you've misjudged a rapid and need to rethink your route, land in the nearest eddy. Landing to shore in big water can be difficult if there are no quiet eddies; you may have to paddle in close and jump out. Make sure the water isn't over your head before you leap. When landing in fast water, it's easiest to join a boat that's already tied up—someone is there to catch your boat, or you can grab onto the other one to avoid being swept down the river.

IKs that don't self-bail may have difficulty maneuvering after becoming swamped by big waves. The quickest way to empty an IK is to land the boat, climb out, and turn the IK upsidedown. If eddies are in short supply, you may need to bail with a scoop—a plastic jug cut open on one side makes a good IK bailer. Or you may want to try the "buddy bump": lean across another paddler, who helps you tip your IK over on one tube, draining the water out the side. Bailing will be difficult if the river is fast and goes right into the next rapid without any slow water for recovery.

In big water, the greatest danger comes from reversals, which swell to enormous proportions. River-runners jokingly describe huge holes as being able to swallow a Greyhound bus, not far from the truth. Avoid these monsters at all cost! If you do find yourself staring down into the maw of a giant hole, take immediate defensive action. Don't turn sideways, hoping to escape, if there isn't enough room to paddle away from it. Going sideways into most any reversal is a one-way ticket out of your IK. Head in bow-first, and paddle like crazy. You want to generate enough speed to punch through the waters curling backward, and power your IK out of the hole. If you fail, you may flip, or find yourself sliding back down into the reversal.

Self-bailers are notorious for becoming stuck in reversals, especially IKs, because the they're so light. A heavy boat often pops right through a hydraulic, and incoming water adds a lot to a boat's weight. Deliberately swamping your boat with water before running big hydraulics used to be a recommended technique for rafters. But if your boat won't fill up with water, you may discover yourself surf-ing—the same as being stuck.

Should you lose momentum, you'll sense the IK sliding back-wards. It'll actually feel as if the river has reached out a hand and grabbed the IK. Brace hard downstream to keep the IK upright, espe-cially if it gets tossed sideways. You may be able to catch the current below the surface with your paddle, and propel the IK free. Some-times the river tires of playing with you and spits you out, but most big reversals won't release an IK until its occupant has been dumped out. Even after you've floated free, the IK may still surf empty for a while, particularly if it is a self-bailer. There's not much you can do except wait for the changing currents to push the boat loose.

The danger of reversals is that strong back currents can easily trap a swimmer, who is then "Maytagged": continually recirculated through the hole until flushed out. This can drown a paddler—a good reason for avoiding reversals. (But even a small hole can kill an unwary paddler, especially the extremely regular hydraulics found below low-head dams.) If you're caught in such a predicament, try not to panic. Remember that the recirculating effect ends at the sides of the reversal; try to work your way out from these sides if you can. If this fails, dive below the surface to reach the forward-flowing cur-rent. Your backup should be there with a throwbag to pull you free. Rescue boaters should be careful not to approach strong hydraulics too closely, even from downstream; the powerful currents may draw their boats into the reversal, too.

Not all big water is this nasty. Many of the large western rivers with reputations for giant rapids, such as the Salmon, aren't difficult to run if you are skilled at reading water and adept at paddling an IK. Big water generally means fewer obstacles to avoid, so paddling may actually be easier. Also keep in mind that river volume varies; you'll find even the huge Colorado tamed by lower-than-normal flows that sometimes occur late in the season.

Flooding can turn any moving water, even a tiny creek, into a raging torrent—often in a matter of hours. While expert hardshell kayakers rub their hands with glee when local rivers flood, IK pad-dlers should wait until rivers drop to a more sensible level. Floods scour the riverbanks, ripping loose logs and uprooting trees, sending these missiles rushing down river. Negotiating a maze of heavy floating timber is very hazardous. Even after the flood waters recede, new strainers may be left behind, posing unknown dangers for boaters. High water pours over boulders previously dry, creating deadly reversals. And even a river you've floated a dozen times will look unfamiliar; you may not recognize landmarks. It may be impossible, with eddies washed out, to find enough calm water to land above rapids. All in all, a flooding river is no place to be in an IK.

What about waterfalls? You may have seen pictures of hardshell kayaks—even IKs—jumping falls. This stunt is only for very experienced boaters who know what they are doing and are willing to assume the risks of falls-jumping. Falls-jumpers need very rigid boats that definitely won't taco on them, plus helmets, and probably a good health insurance policy. The accepted technique is to paddle at full speed as you approach the dropoff, so that the boat will clear any ledges, rocks, and dangerous hydraulics below. Small drops over ledges offer saner ways to test jumping abilities, unless there are hazardous reversals lurking below.

5

SAFETY ON MOVING WATER

Whitewater conjures up frightening images of angry rapids that rip you out of your little boat and dash you against the rocks. In reality, running whitewater is considerably safer than driving down a typical American highway. Especially when whitewater is run intelligently, rather than haphazardly. Besides understanding how river currents work, there are special techniques that whitewater boaters can use to keep themselves out of trouble, or to get out of trouble should something go wrong. Learn these techniques, and commit the rules of moving water safety to memory.

SELF-RESCUE

The most important technique every IK paddler must know— even flatwater boaters—is how to perform self-rescue. Before you undertake a trip, practice self-rescue until you fully understand the technique. Before you paddle an IK that you're not used to, practice self-rescue in calm water, so you understand the differences between your regular IK and the new boat. Self-rescue is important because when you paddle an IK, you are on your own. Even with other paddlers around you, or a support raft nearby, it's much easier for you to rescue yourself than to depend on someone else. You'll be out of the water faster, with less risk of injury, if you can promptly execute self-rescue whenever you fall out of or overturn your IK. Self-rescue is the IK paddler's version of the Eskimo roll; although not as elegant, it serves the same function: it gets you back upright and paddling once more.

First, remember to hold onto your paddle should you flip or spill out of your IK. That's one less thing to worry about saving later on, and besides, you're going to need it once you're back in the boat. Should you lose your paddle, but not your boat, you may be able to paddle the IK to shore with your hands, or swim it there. But don't try this in heavy water. If you can't land the boat safely, leave it. People come first, equipment is second!

Next, look for your boat. Nine times out of ten, you'll emerge right next to the IK. Grab hold of it! Many paddlers become so disoriented by a swim that they fail to locate their IK, even though it's right beside them. When you swim, don't panic! Going out of the boat isn't as terrible as you think it is, if you keep your cool.

This is where handholds and flip straps earn their keep. The bottom of any IK will be smooth and slippery—difficult to hold. Before

Performing self-rescue with an inflatable kayak. First, make sure you have the paddle at hand. Next, turn the IK upright by using the flip strap.

Put the paddle inside the IK, and use the flip strap to pull yourself over the tubes and back inside the IK.

you're alongside it in cold water, you should be familiar with the bottom of your particular breed of IK. Are their good-sized drain holes cut into the bottom? Fine—latch onto those. Short grab loops or big D-rings at bow and stern also offer good handholds. Some paddlers reach underneath an overturned IK and hang onto the thwart, spray shield, or seat. If you've fastened a flip strap around the IK, you have a good handle conveniently located.

Once you have hold of the IK (and, presumably, your paddle), exert enough force to pull the boat back upright. A tug on a flip strap accomplishes this quickly. If the boat is empty, it'll be easy to right from just about anywhere; if you have a heavy load, you may have to swim the boat to shore or into an eddy. Sometimes, the IK empties itself of a paddler without overturning; in this case, retain the paddle, hold onto a tube, and haul yourself in.

Getting back into the upright IK is a matter of pulling yourself over the flotation tubes. You'll want to put the paddle back inside first. Approach the IK from the upstream side, keeping it in front of you, and enter over one of the sides, not from the ends (especially if cargo or spray shields are in the way). Reach across the IK and try pulling yourself back in at the same time. If you don't succeed the first time, pull again, and kick hard like a frog for additional leverage. Again, a flip strap helps with re-entry, especially if you don't have sufficient arm strength to pull your weight into the boat.

If all else fails, push the IK between your legs and scramble aboard over bow or stern.

If, after several tries, you just can't get back into the IK over the side tubes, push the front end of the IK between your legs and wiggle up on your belly—it's awkward but it works, especially when climbing back aboard IKs with big side tubes.

Once you're settled back in the seat, grab your paddle and resume the run.

The best place to learn self-rescue is a heated swimming pool. Check with local paddling clubs to see if community pools are available (hardshell kayakers may have a time set aside for practicing their Eskimo rolls). Lacking a convenient swimming pool, try a pond or quiet inlet of a lake. Wear your life jacket, and take your paddle along, so you can practice under realistic conditions. When you can successfully perform a self-rescue on flatwater, try it on moving water. Many IK paddlers learn this technique the hard way, after being dumped in whitewater for the first time. Besides giving you the skills to get out of the water faster, mastering self-rescue beforehand gives you a boost in confidence.

What if you can't get back into the IK right away? Then you want to keep the boat in front of you, so there's no chance of being wedged between it and a rock—although, because the IK is light, it seldom poses much of a threat. If you can't re-enter in midriver, work the IK to shore, or to an eddy, where another paddler may be around to assist you.

ASSISTED RESCUES

Every paddler should be ready to use the backup, or buddy, system to assist another boater in trouble. When another paddler

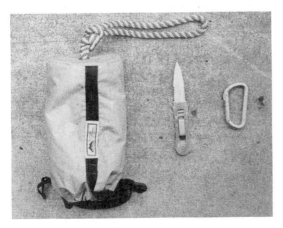

Basic river emergency gear: throwbag, river knife, carabiner.

dumps and is separated from his or her IK, or has trouble getting back in, a rescue boat should intervene. Approach a spilled paddler carefully, especially someone not in your group. Some people panic after a spill in cold water, and in their fear can pull your IK over. Try to maneuver in front of the swimmer, so you can be seen, and shout encouragement such as, "You're doing fine," or "I'm coming to get you." Ideally, a swimmer should hold onto your IK and be towed to shore. Or, if the empty boat is nearby, return the swimmer to it and help him or her get back in. However, if another rapid is coming up fast, or if the swimmer is cold or hurt, it's better to get him or her inside your boat, and to shore. A swimmer can be carried across the back of your IK, but use caution; the extra weight can throw you off balance. Have the person lay flat across the tubes behind you, and not sit up until you reach flatwater. Keeping weight low in the boat minimizes the chance of upsets.

Backup boats should wait in a convenient rescue spot, such as an eddy, just below rapids where others are likely to flip. In this position, you're ready to paddle out and intercept a swimmer immediately. Backups can also operate from shore, using a throwbag to assist swimmers. The throwbag is a length of floating rope stuffed into a nylon bag, which is equipped with foam flotation. Basically, the throwbag extends a rescuer's reach. To throw the bag, open the drawstring closure and pull out the free end of the rope, which has a loop for a handhold and a knot to keep it inside the bag when not in use. Leave the drawstring open so the rope will feed out. Hang onto the looped end, then throw the bag towards the swimmer. Aim for a spot in front of the swimmer, so the rope can be seen, remembering that the current will move both rope and swimmer as you toss. Shout "Rope in front of you!" so the swimmer will know the rope is there. Rescue ropes should be bright orange for best visibility in the water.

Swimmers should grab the *rope* at that point, not the *bag*. If the bag is snatched, the rope continues to feed out, delaying the rescue. And NEVER tie or loop the rope around yourself; just hold onto it with both hands. Should you get caught in the rope, you risk becoming trapped underwater. When the rescuer begins to pull the rope towards shore, the swimmer should float on his or her back, not stomach-down, as that position plows the face through the water. If you miss the swimmer, reel the rope back in, making large coils as you go, and throw it again. *Always* remember to hold onto the loose end of the rope when you toss a throwbag.

After the rescue, the rope must be stuffed back into the bag carefully, so it'll be ready the next time you need it. Close the drawstring almost all the way, then feed the line back in slowly, a little bit at a time. Rope crammed back into the bag will undoubtedly tangle and be useless for the next rescue. This restuffing takes a few minutes to do correctly, but the time is well spent. It's also worthwhile to practice tossing a throwbag, so you have the technique down. Some boaters prefer to throw the bag overhand, others like the underhand toss. In practice sessions, toss a small stick out into the water, then try to aim the rope to "save" the stick.

A throwbag is the safest way to rescue someone in nasty rapids where you wouldn't want to paddle back in, or swim in. However, you need to be careful with the loose rope. Never use a throwbag if the person can be more easily rescued some other way. Certainly, don't throw a line to someone engaged in a self-rescue—the rope could entangle them.

HOW TO SWIM A RAPID

If you become separated from your IK in a rapid, don't panic. Look around. If it's fairly close, and no obstacles are coming up right

When a paddler dumps out of an IK stuck in reversal, the empty IK may continue to surf, but it will usually wash out in a few moments.

away, swim over to the IK and proceed with self-rescue. If you're approaching rocks or waves, forget the IK and position your body for rough-water swimming. Sit in the water, with your feet off the bottom and floating in front of you. Never swim if there are rocks ahead—just let your life jacket float you in the sitting position. This way, you can ward off oncoming rocks with your feet instead of your head. (This is the reason you're wearing tennis shoes or hard-soled booties.) Use your arms in a backstroke to position yourself in the rapid. Float on your back in the sitting position, enjoy the ride, and worry about recovering your IK at the bottom of the rapid.

Remember: don't try to swim whitewater in the traditional fashion of head-first locomotion, because it's too easy to clunk your head on a rock. The only exceptions are bad hazards coming up fast (in which case you should head for shore) or strainers directly in your path. If you see a strainer this close to you, go HEAD FIRST and try to grab onto the branches so you don't get sucked under. Otherwise, always float feet first, backpaddling with your arms for control.

Don't try to stand up in a moving current, even if the water is very shallow. Swift waters can easily knock you over. If your feet are on the bottom of the river, they could become pinned under a rock, and if the current pushed your head under, you could drown—even in two feet of water. So let the life jacket do its job, at least until you are safely back in your boat or right next to shore.

Incidentally, this swimming through whitewater is quite popular among whitewater boaters, who call it bodysurfing and readily throw themselves into the top of a clean rapid so they can float through big waves. At the bottom, they swim to shore, walk back upriver, and go through again. Besides being fun, bodysurfing an easy rapid allows you the opportunity to sample rough water swimming, so you'll be less likely to panic when it happens for real. Just make sure there aren't any rocks lurking under the surface, and that there's plenty of calm water at the bottom to get out of the river. Also wear your PFD and shoes for this! Usually you need to swim out to the middle of the rapid, where the tongue will carry you into the waves. Take a breath as you are carried into the trough of the wave. When the current lifts you up to the crest, hold your breath. Depending on how large it is, the wave will probably come crashing over your head, inhibiting breathing for several seconds. Repeat for each successive wave. A responsible person should wait below the bodysurfing wave with a boat or throwbag to pull back any exhausted swimmers in danger of being swept downstream.

PROTECTIVE CLOTHING

Always wear adequate clothing to protect against cold water and sunburn; always wear protective foot gear (tennis shoes or wetsuit booties); strap on glasses to prevent loss; wear sunglasses and a hat to cut down on glare and increase visibility of rocks. In very rocky waters, wear a helmet and wetsuit.

The biggest threat presented by the river environment is hypothermia, a condition in which the body loses heat faster than it can be generated and which can result in death if the heat loss isn't stopped. If you dump in very cold water, get out immediately, even if this means crawling on top of your overturned boat, or abandoning your boat to swim for shore. Even with protective clothing, hypothermia can set in quickly.

ENTRAPMENT

It sounds very nasty, and it is. Entrapment occurs whenever a boater is trapped underwater. The combination of a river current (even a slow current) and an entangling object can prove fatal. Boaters on moving water must be alert for possible entrapment situations: strainers and logs, loose ropes, underwater caves, and undercut rocks in swift currents. Give these obstacles a wide berth.

Never tie yourself into a boat on moving water, and never (except on an ocean or a lake) attach a line between the boat and yourself or the paddle. When being rescued by a throw line, or when swimming whitewater, never wrap or tie a line around any part of your body. Avoid encumbrances like cameras or binoculars around your neck. Secure all loose lines and have cargo tied down with straps that are just long enough to do the job, without extra length flapping around. Carry a diver's survival knife and know how to use it to cut yourself free. A knife with serrated edges will quickly saw through most ropes.

SAFETY IN NUMBERS

Never boat alone—stay with an IK group or support raft. Also, when running rapids, don't just think about yourself; watch out for your boating buddies. The most experienced boater should lead the group, demonstrating the best route through each rapid and waiting below as the rest of the paddlers come through. The second-most experienced boater should run as a "sweep" boat behind the group to make sure everyone gets through each run and that nobody gets left behind. Inexperienced boaters should never pass the lead boat. Before embarking on an expedition, file a float plan with a responsible person, so someone will search if you're long overdue.

EMERGENCY GEAR

Carry basic emergency gear and know how to use it. This includes a spare breakdown paddle for the group, in case someone breaks a paddle. For major expeditions, each IK should carry a throwbag for rescuing swimmers or pulling boats off rocks. (This rope also comes in handy for erecting clotheslines, tarps, and so forth. Special kayak throwbags are available from river supply stores.) Among the group's gear, there should be at least two air pumps, in case one is lost or breaks down. The party also needs a good repair kit and a first-aid kit. Individual paddlers, especially in cold weather or wilderness situations, should carry some kind of survival kit on their person, with a fire starter, such as a candle or road flare, matches in a waterproof container, a rescue carabiner, and a signal whistle. Most kayakers carry a diver's knife attached to their PFD so it's instantly available to cut an entangling rope, even underwater.

AVOIDING TROUBLE

Never boat water beyond your ability. Sometimes the good sense to portage is the better part of valor. When faced with a rapid that appears too tough for you or your group, there are alternatives. First of all, you can portage, or carry the IK, around the rapid. (If you are carrying gear, it's easiest to unload this and carry it separately, or to have two people carry the loaded IK—one holding each end. Two light IKs can also be carried in similar fashion—stack one on top of the other, then grab the ends of the bottom IK).

Another alternative to running a rapid is to guide, or line, the boat down the shallows next to shore. Two lines are attached to the loaded IK, one on the bow and one on the stern, and held secure by two people on the shore. The person with the bow line leads the boat downriver, while the person with the stern line pays out the rope slowly, acting as brake and anchor to keep the IK from getting out of control. When lining a boat, always wear your life jacket and never wrap the rope around yourself. An IK is very light and shouldn't get carried away in the current like a heavy raft might. If more control is necessary, belay the line around a tree trunk or a smooth rock.

WHAT TO DO IF STRANDED

The best way to avoid becoming stranded on the river is to keep your party together and stay out of sticky situations. If your IK gets away from you and is washed downstream, get to shore. Another member of your party should be able to recover it, or you may be able to catch up with it in an eddy downstream. Don't play guessing games with your companions—if you become separated, signal (blast on your whistle) to let them know you're OK. If you are injured or stranded out of sight of your party, signal the emergency with three blasts on your whistle, repeated at regular intervals (three of anything—whistles, smoke plumes, etc.—are universal signals of distress).

It's not uncommon for boaters on a day trip to become stranded overnight for one reason or another. Consequently, whenever you head out for a "short, easy trip" down a river, carry a survival kit. How extensive such a kit should be depends on how remote and difficult the river is. At the minimum, you should carry waterproof matches (and maybe a lighter) and something to boost a balky fire. (There are special firestarters available, or you can use candles.) A fire will allow you to stay out overnight, and serves as a signal for rescuers, in addition to providing emergency warming of hypothermia victims. Something for shelter should always be carried. Several options for a lightweight, compact emergency shelter are a small nylon tarp, a tube tent, or a space blanket. If you find yourself stuck without shelter, sleeping under a propped-up IK works well in most weather. If there's a removable cushion or floor, use this for padding and insulation underneath you; or use your PFD to protect your body from the ground. Emergency rations, first aid and repair kit, pump, signal device (whistle), and a knife should also be carried on every trip, no matter how short. In addition to carrying such gear, study basic survival techniques.

A paddler can be stranded if his or her IK should become lost on, or stuck in, the river. Except on rivers with strong current, an IK that floats away is seldom gone forever. Walk downstream several miles, preferably with one person on each side of the river, to search for a missing IK before giving it up as lost. Many missing boats will show up in downstream eddies, as will paddles or other gear that floated away. If you lose anything, keep alert as you continue down the river. Also, you should mark your IK and gear, so that if there is any confusion about ownership, you can identify what's yours. If your IK comes with a serial number patch installed, record this number and carry it in your wallet for quick reference. Otherwise, write your name and address on everything, using a waterproof felt marker. Most paddlers are honest and will return items they find, if they have a way to discern the owner and find his or her address easily. Also, an owner's name clearly visible on gear will help discourage theft, especially of things like PFDs which otherwise tend to look alike.

A self-bailer can dump its paddler, then become stuck in river hydraulics. Eventually, it will work loose and float downriver. You may be able to toss something like a rock onto the IK and knock it free, or another boater may push it free.

ROCKSIDE

Wrapping an IK around a rock or cliff wall is a different matter entirely. Learn how rocks appear in moving water, and work to avoid them whenever possible; don't hit them just because the inflatable bounces off. Some rocks are practically unavoidable. Paddlers need to be alert for wrap situations, so these can be avoided, if possible, and be ready to take corrective action. Besides larger boul-

When broaching sideways on a rock is unavoidable, lean toward the rock. Never shrink away from an obstacle!

ders, IKs may wrap against cliff walls, log jams, logs pinned by the current against rocks, and bridge pillars.

Try not to broadside a rock or other obstacle; if you're headed directly for a big boulder, pivot to hit bow-on. If you hit sideways, lean TOWARD the rock and brace toward the rock with your paddle (this maneuver is called "rockside"). This lifts the upstream tube of the IK higher, so that water will rush underneath, not inside, the boat; this often pushes the IK free of the obstacle. NEVER cringe away from the obstacle—this just makes the situation worse. If caught broadside in a near-wrap situation, don't get out of the IK until all hope is lost—keep leaning! Be wary of entrapment, however, when faced with a wrap situation; prepare to abandon the IK to the river, if necessary, so you won't get trapped. If the IK starts to wrap, get loose and climb onto the rock.

Wrapped IKs are not held down with as much force as are larger inflatables, and usually won't require complicated rescue techniques, unless your rescue crew lacks muscle power. It may be necessary to open a valve and release air pressure from one or both side tubes, or from an inflatable floor, in order to free the IK. Sometimes cutting the floor out may help (another reason to always carry a river knife on whitewater rivers). If your IK is damaged beyond repair—a remote possibility—you may be able to ride out with another paddler (gear may have to be unloaded) or with another river party. If not, you may have to walk out.

IKs are not as prone to wrapping around rocks as are bigger inflatables—stiffer IKs, especially those with ethafoam floors, resist wrapping more than less-rigid models—but if it happens, don't give up. Attach rescue lines through the sturdiest part of the IK—the drain holes on a self-bailer, the thwart, or the D-rings—and start pulling. If the force of the river is too strong, try to increase your mechanical advantage with a Z-drag (a good book to consult for this procedure is *River Rescue*—see Appendix).

In wrap situations or other emergencies, boaters can become stranded on midstream rocks, waiting for rescue. In really rough water, a swimmer may be better off to head for the nearest rock rather than go for shore or attempt to ride the entire rapid without a boat. However a paddler arrives at a boulder, getting off poses problems. The best rescue boat is a raft, but rafts are not always available and can't always land in the small eddies found below many river rocks. Another IK paddler may approach, but should use caution; an overeager victim leaping onto a vulnerable IK can cause a capsize or impede maneuverability. The best approach is to present the stern and have the victim hold on without getting in, if possible, or lay over the tubes, keeping his or her weight low. A bigger IK without gear in the stern compartment can accommodate a victim sitting up, but the swimmer needs to climb in carefully, so as not to unbalance the boater. Sometimes a person stranded on a rock is best rescued by a throwbag from shore. Remind swimmers not to tie the line around themselves.

By the way, rock-sitters must exercise restraint when getting off the rock. Never leap from the rock into the water or onto another boat—you can injure yourself badly attempting this stunt. Always lower yourself carefully into the water or rescue boat. If no boat comes, rock-sitters must consider swimming to shore if the water isn't numbing cold, and if the whitewater isn't too fierce. Otherwise, stay put and wait a while longer.

GETTING HELP IN EMERGENCIES

On a river trip, you're on your own. Your group must be self-sufficient, even if there are other parties on the river. Not everyone knows how to help other boaters who get into trouble, and unfortunately, not everyone will stop and offer assistance. Should a serious injury occur, you must take charge.

First of all, calm and treat the injured person to the best of your ability. Making a decision about what to do next may be the hardest part, unless you have expert medical advice available. But you must decide on the best course of action. If you're close to civilization, someone can walk to a road and flag down a car. If there are others on the river, they can send for help. Big commercial parties may have doctors among their guests, and some have emergency transmitters. Commercial outfitters can also float an injured person out on a large raft, if immediate evacuation is necessary. Jet boats and other motorized craft may be a nuisance for paddlers in search of solitude, but they offer a quick route back to civilization. To flag down other boaters, use universal river distress signals: wave a PFD or blast on your whistle (these are understood by most floaters, but not always by motorboaters).

Houses and lodges may be located along some rivers, but seek help in these places in serious situations only. Phones may not be available in wilderness areas. Government officials such as park rangers can also provide emergency assistance for paddlers, and usually have radios. Evacuation from a remote or inaccessible canyon usually requires a helicopter—look for a good landing site and mark the spot, or have someone standing by with brightly colored clothing to wave.

You should review your trip beforehand, making sure everyone in the party knows where potential evacuation and hike-out sites are located. Before you leave, file a float plan with a responsible party, so would-be rescuers will know where to look for you in case your trip is delayed by an accident.

Lessons in general first aid and CPR are a good idea before wilderness expeditions. Chances are you'll never use most of the skills, but should you need them, you'll be glad you took the time to learn. Your local Red Cross chapter holds year-round classes. However, these mainly teach skills for rescues in big cities. You may find more useful wilderness "second aid" skills (those needed to sustain life and treat injuries in emergencies when no doctor is readily available) taught in some community college outdoor programs, or consult one of the many excellent wilderness medicine books on the shelf. On really remote trips, inviting a doctor who paddles isn't a bad idea.

For lesser injuries, the victim may be capable of paddling. Set a slow, comfortable pace, and don't force the person beyond his or her capabilities. Take frequent rests and give plenty of encouragement. Have a stronger paddler take the victim's boat through any major rapids, while the victim walks around. It's also possible to have another paddler take a moderately injured person down the river in the stern compartment of a K-2 boat. Redistribute gear among the group to lighten the rescue boat's load, or leave it behind if there's no room for it. The victim's IK may also have to be left behind, if carrying it will overload other boats. Deflate the IK and roll it up, then stash it in the bushes. You can always come back for it later, or ask another float group to pick it up for you. Remember, people come first, then equipment.

DECISION MAKING

Anytime someone is hurt—except in cases of minor injuries—another person should examine the victim immediately. Don't allow the victim to walk around, or shrug off an injury as "nothing" until someone knowledgeable has taken a good look. Be alert for signs of shock (which indicate a major injury): pale complexion, fast pulse or breathing, skin sweaty yet clammy, nausea, light-headedness. If you suspect shock, treat the injury, then treat for shock. Have the victim lie down and elevate the legs, if this can be done comfortably (you may be able to use an IK). Keep the victim warm with sleeping bags or whatever else may be handy (such as a space blanket on a day trip).

A qualified person must make the decision to evacuate a victim or continue on. This is where first aid training pays for itself. Generally, don't count on the victim being able to make this decision. Emotions can get in the way of responsible decision making—the victim doesn't want to ruin everyone else's good time, or has been planning this trip for years, etc. It's better to evacuate for a minor injury than to keep on going with an undiagnosed condition.

On major expeditions, designate a leader—an experienced person with solid first aid training—whose job is to make such decisions. Other trained persons can assist the leader in decision making by offering their opinions, but the final call is up to the leader. On more casual trips, everyone should agree to a course of action, with the needs of any injured person taking precedence over the trip.

PLANNING

Proper planning can eliminate many problems. When you plan the time you'll be spending on an expedition, remember flexibility. Allow sufficient time for the trip you have planned, so that you don't feel pressured to make miles. Pushing too hard downstream can cause fatigue and lead to accidents. Remember that rivers move at their own pace—they're not for anyone who's in a hurry to get somewhere.

Should the river rise unexpectedly, and you have extra time in your schedule, you can wait for it to drop down to a safer level. Or, if an IK is ripped, you can pull over and make camp, and have ample time for the glue to dry. Should the wind blow harder upriver than you anticipated, cutting your daily miles in half, you won't have to strain as hard, knowing you have extra time to complete the float. Unexpected delays can add hours or days to a float. Always allow extra time (and food) to cover possible delays.

Preplanning eliminates guesswork about rapids. Find out everything you can about a new river before you go; what you don't know can hurt you. Always scout major rapids before running them, even if you've seen them before. Rapids change from season to season, and you never know if a log has washed downriver and lodged in the rapid until you take a look.

Likewise, always be prepared for bad weather and hypothermia, even if your expedition is down a desert river in August. A hypothermic person may not be able to recognize and deal with their condition, so other members of the party must assume that function. A paddler who is cold and tired may make foolish mistakes. Plan to stop and rest if someone becomes tired or cold. And never run serious rapids unless you're ready for them, physically and mentally.

RESPECT THE RIVER

A moving current possesses tremendous force. Paddlers need to respect this force. Even on easy waters, keep your eyes open for obstacles. Rocks just below the surface, known as sleepers, are particularly tricky, because they can't be seen until you're almost on top of them. Also watch out for strainers, log jams, logs pinned against rocks, and other downed wood; the current runs deceptively swift into and under many of these. An unwary IK can be sucked into this current, so give all timber a wide berth.

On many rivers, the most dangerous obstacles are man-made. Low-head dams, found along many rivers close to civilization, are

In a rapid, keep your cool. These paddlers need to lean to the high (upper) side to avert a flip, but they aren't working together. Remember, the most important item of river equipment is your head!

lethal for small boats, because a swimmer can become trapped in the hydraulics created by the smooth, unbroken drop. Unlike natural hydraulics, there may not be an escape route from the low-head dam. Be alert for a sudden change of elevation ahead—if the horizon line drops off abruptly, pull over to shore and investigate. This could indicate a low-head dam, a waterfall, or an unrunnable rapid. Don't ignore a big roar ahead just because your map or previous experience says there's no rapid. Heavy rains can make giant rapids appear overnight. Always carry your boat around dams and other big drops. Other hazards are bridge piers, which can pin an unwary IK paddler, and barbed wire fences in the river.

Start making your move to shore well above a falls or other obstacle. When trying to land, you may find the current to be stronger than it looks, and your IK could get carried away. Get into the habit of using a strong upstream ferry to land, even in easy, quiet water, so when the pressure is on, you can land with room to spare.

IKs usually do better in clean rapids, big waves, and low water than in heavy hydraulics. Low water lessens the power of a river's flow, so late summer is a good time to learn about rocks and currents. Sure, there are lots of rocks, but there's also more time to avoid them.

STAYING OUT OF TROUBLE

Try to stay in the IK. Learn the strokes and leans that keep you in the boat. Also remember the importance of the rockside technique. These techniques will save you many swims. You are much safer staying in the boat than swimming through whitewater. Too many paddlers give up in whitewater. Keep paddling!

Should the IK be caught on a rock or stuck on a gravel bar, be careful getting out of the boat to push it loose. Try to wiggle free first. Get out and push only as a last resort, but if you do get out, keep a hand on the IK while you're pushing. Don't let strong currents tear the IK away from you. Nothing is more embarrassing than standing in the middle of a shallow river and watching your boat float away from you. When pushing off, watch out for deep water and slippery rocks.

If your IK doesn't self-bail, you'll need to dump out the water that splashes inside to avoid losing maneuverability. A plastic jug cut open on one side makes a good IK bailer. With lots of water, you may be better off pulling over to shore and dumping the whole boat upsidedown. (This is difficult, of course, with a load of gear inside, in which case you'll want to push the loaded stern onto a patch of sand so that the lighter bow sits lower, thereby draining all the water down to one spot for easier scooping.) You can empty some water from your boat by leaning across another paddler's boat while he or she helps you tip yours up on one side tube; this is easier than constantly stopping and getting out of the boat.

DEALING WITH HEAVY HYDRAULICS

IK paddlers should avoid holes and other fierce river currents until they have gained the skill and experience necessary to deal with these strong currents. However, should your boat be caught in a reversal, there are several things you can do.

If a hole looms ahead, unavoidably, never enter sideways. Go in bow-first, paddling like the devil is after you. Keep paddling as long as you can. At the first sign of begin knocked backwards or sideways, lean and brace your paddle downstream.

Remember that self-bailers surf in reversals. Highside and brace to prevent dumping. Stay with the boat if dumped—an IK offers more flotation than your PFD. To swim out of a reversal, dive below the turbulence or swim to one side. Tucking into a ball may help. In a desperate situation—when you're trapped by the hydraulic of a low-head dam, for example—dive to the bottom, hang onto the rocks, and crawl away. Other boaters can rescue a trapped paddler from a safe distance using a throwbag rope. Never paddle or swim back into a reversal to rescue someone—you can become trapped yourself! If you find yourself heading into a reversal while swimming, take in as much air as you can, then curl up into a ball as you enter.

6

BACKPACKING BY BOAT
Inflatable Kayak Camping

The only thing better than a day on the river is two days on the river—or three. IKs are excellent for camping. You can get away from roads and civilization without the strain of backpacking or the nuisance of pack animals. You can go where there is no trail, yet leave not a trace of your passage behind, save for some footprints in the sand. You can go with bigger boats for support, enjoying a luxurious camp, or you can paddle away from the crowds on waterways too small for other boats.

Until you gain experience in paddling and packing, you'll probably want to have a support raft along to haul your gear and escort you down the river. More skill is necessary to paddle with a load, and to pack the load into a small space. In addition, more care is necessary in selecting gear for an all-IK trip. With an IK, each item you take must be carefully considered—take only the most versatile, useful, rugged, lightweight, and compact items.

It sounds like a lot of work, but the rewards of all-IK expeditions—the freedom to go where you want, when you want, enjoying solitude and wildlife—are well worth the effort involved.

EQUIPMENT FOR IK CAMPING

The type of equipment needed for IK camping depends on whether a support boat will accompany the group. With a raft to carry all or most of your gear, there are few limitations on bulk or weight of the gear, other than the cooperation and skill of the support boat person and the size of the raft. Most any kind of tent and sleeping bag will do in this case, because weight and water resistance aren't as important. Remember, gear carried high on a raft stays relatively dry. It's not so much the constant spray from whitewater that forces dry bags to leak, but sitting *in* water, especially around the bag's seal. If your IK isn't self-bailing, a cargo bag may be sitting in water much of the day. Even if the water drains out of the boat quickly, the bag will still be wetter than one sitting high on a big raft. When selecting gear for all-IK trips, keep this in mind. Everything going into a bag carried on an IK in whitewater should be double-sealed, and gear should be selected with water resistance in mind. For example, there are some very dependable waterproof flashlights on the market these days. Why risk ruining a regular flashlight when, for a little bit more, you can own a waterproof one?

For all-IK trips, you need gear that is both lightweight and not very bulky, so everything will fit into the boat without overloading it. Standard backpackers' tents work very well for IK camping, as do most hiker sleeping bags. How much weight you can carry in your IK depends on several factors: the size of your boat, your own body weight, how hard you want to paddle, and how difficult the river is. Obviously, you can carry a much bigger load on an easy stream that has only a few Class II rapids to negotiate, while on a very technical outing, you want to go lighter. Most important, never overload your boat on trips when you must be able to make quick maneuvers and sharp turns, or if you must make frequent portages. On big whitewater, extra weight may give you stability in the heavy hydraulics, but it may also make the IK harder to turn upright after a flip.

Group paddlers don't need one of everything; plan on sharing cookstoves, fuel, air pumps, first aid kits, and so forth so that less gear is required. Consolidating meals, if everyone can agree on the same foods, also cuts down on weight and bulk.

Tents: Pro and Con

Shelter is usually necessary for a comfortable night out, unless you plan to camp on a tropical beach. This means a tent for most people. But, while tents offer many advantages, they aren't mandatory for wilderness comfort. Sleeping under the stars is an almost forgotten pastime these days, with high-tech domes popping out everywhere. A surprising number of people cling to the belief that sleeping in a tent is mandatory when camping. People inevitably hide in their tents all night, especially in developed campgrounds. In such places, tents do offer valuable privacy. But the habit is hard to break, even when you're out on a wilderness river where your nearest neighbor is miles downstream. If you've never tried sleeping out, you're in for a real treat. For your first time, choose a warm summer night, with clear skies and a gentle breeze blowing. You don't want to become chilled or get rained on that first time.

Tents, of course, offer great bug-proofing. In areas where ticks, chiggers, mosquitoes, and other pests are a problem, a good tent with screening tight enough to keep out even the no-see-ums is a blessing. Another option for buggy areas is using just netting for your outdoor canopy. This allows good ventilation and views of the stars, while preventing intrusion by small biting menaces. Some quite elaborate netting affairs, complete with poles, can be acquired for those who like sleeping out but hate bugs. Surprisingly enough, many rivers—such as those flowing through western desertlands—don't present bug problems. You need sluggish backwater for breeding mosquitoes, and along a swift stream, there isn't much habitat for these pesky biters. And cool canyon breezes often blow at night, sweeping bugs away.

Tents keep bigger nocturnal creatures away from you, as well. In snake country, sleeping in a tent is a good idea, even if only for peace of mind. Some folks just can't deal with the thought of wild creatures wandering freely around them while they sleep. Erecting a tent—or perhaps a hammock—is much easier than trying to change this attitude.

Another advantage tents offer is additional warmth during a cold night. And tent walls block wind as well as rain. After a hard day of fighting upstream winds, it's a relief to climb into a tent and get out of that blasted breeze.

A good compromise is the personal sleep shelter, or bivouac, offered by camping outfitters. Resembling a large fabric envelope, these shelters are very light in weight, take up little space in an IK, and are almost as good as tents for keeping out cold and rain. Most good ones have bug screening, too. These give you the feel of sleeping out without the hassles.

Especially in desert areas, many boaters like to carry a tarp for shelter. This is nothing more than a big sheet of plastic (construction-quality Visqueen is strong) or nylon, sometimes with metal grommets in strategic locations, which the camper pitches like a tent without walls. Tarps keep rain off you during the night, and unlike a tent, won't trap moisture from your body inside. Tarps actually keep you drier and more comfortable than cheap, poorly made tents, which may drown you and your sleeping bag in condensation. A tarp can be pitched just about anywhere, using handy trees or bushes for support. In open country, use paddles or even your IK to support the shelter. A compact nylon tarp is worth carrying along on short trips, just in case you unexpectedly get caught out overnight. Also, a tarp pitched between trees or on paddles creates a dry spot for food preparation during a deluge.

For increased comfort when sleeping out with no shelter, you will need some kind of sleeping bag cover that allows moisture to evaporate and separates you from the damp ground underneath. Similar to the personal bivouac shelter, this envelope of fabric increases the warmth of your sleeping bag and protects it from dirt and damage. These "bivy sacks" can hold your air mattress or pad inside them, too, preventing the cushion from sliding out from underneath you.

Underneath tents, tarps, or sleeping bags, many campers like to use a ground cloth. This acts as a moisture barrier to keep the sleeping area drier. Remember that the ground around a waterway is likely to be damp—some kind of ground cloth is usually necessary. Most any kind of plastic or nylon will work. Inside a tent, an extra layer of waterproofing, such as a space blanket, helps cut down on moisture from condensation, and adds a bit of insulation for colder nights.

Sleeping Bags for IK Trips

Forget down-filled sleeping bags. While great for hikers who need the light weight and compactability of down, these bags are just too unreliable for IK camping. The problem with down is that it's totally useless when wet. As inherently wet boats, IKs are no place for down sleeping bags—even sealed in miles of plastic. Even off the river, a sleeping bag can get wet from water vapor, and there's a lot of vapor floating around in the night air around any waterway.

These days, quality synthetic bags are almost as good as down, both in warmth for their weight and in their ability to be stuffed into a small bundle. Bags made of Hollofil or PolarGuard are the best choices for IK camping. If they get wet, most of the moisture can be squeezed out, and the bags will still offer a good degree of lifesaving warmth. They can be dried out by placing them on a warm rock, or hanging them in a breeze, or, with care, near a campfire. They are easier to wash than down sleeping bags and don't need to be fluffed before you can sleep in them.

Even though your synthetic bag can be used wet or easily dried, you should pack it with the same care you'd give to a down bag. If the bag has collected moisture by morning—perhaps from a heavy dew—try to dry it out before you pack it away. Shake the bag out to get rid of sand, which accumulates everywhere when you beach camp. Always keep your bag inside its stuff sack, which affords a good measure of protection against dirt and moisture. Seal the sleeping bag inside a heavy-duty lawn-and-leaf or garbage bag, then place this in the lower part of the dry bag (the most secure spot, because most leaks occur around the seal at the top).

How heavy should the sleeping bag be for IK camping? This depends on the kind of conditions you expect to encounter. The best bag will be heavy enough to let you sleep out in a variety of climates, without being so heavy that you roast on summer trips. You can always unzip a warm bag, or sleep on top of it, but it's uncomfortable, and possibly dangerous, to be stuck out overnight in a less-than-adequate sleeping bag. Generally, a bag with two to three pounds of synthetic fill will serve for most camping conditions encountered between late spring and early fall. A liner or a second, lighter bag inside the main bag will increase the bag's warmth. Polar fleece liners work well and eliminate the clammy feel of a nylon sleeping bag. And you can always wear warm clothing to bed on a cold night. In really cold weather, use a heavy sleeping bag temperature-rated to the conditions you expect, or two medium weight bags—one nestled inside the other.

Consider, also, that the climate of a river is unique. Often, the temperature at the bottom of a deep canyon may be considerably warmer than at the top; it may be snowing on the North Rim of the Grand Canyon, but not along the Colorado River at the bottom. At the same time, that desert canyon can cool off quickly at night, and breezes coming off the cold water of the river can create an unexpected chill, even on summer trips. Nights may be expected to warm up as you drift down a river, as the elevation is dropping with every mile: a cold night at the put-in scares many boaters into taking much more warm gear than they need a night or two later.

Sleeping Cushions

While outdoor enthusiasts continue to debate the relative merits of the air mattress versus the foam pad versus the self-inflating pad, IK campers have little choice. Those nice ensolite foam pads and

Therma-Rests are just a little too bulky to fit inside most IKs, although you *can* use them if you have a larger IK and pack carefully. Air mattresses, which fold down into compact little bundles, are a better choice. If you have a good air mattress and use it properly, you'll sleep far better than you ever would on some skinny little pad.

The problem with air mattresses is that they leak. In fact, they're so notorious for leaking air that they give all inflatables a bad rap. Air mattresses are usually designed for the sunbathing and swimming pool crowd. Consequently, serious campers are often stuck with cheap, vinyl air mattresses that can be punctured by a lousy pine needle, or worse, that burst of their own accord. The solution would be to have an air mattress that is made from the same coated fabric as a good IK. Such a mattress would last for ten years or more, and could be tossed down anywhere without fear of sharp objects. Unfortunately, nobody makes an air mattress like this for camping, because it would be horribly expensive, probably costing nearly $100. Of course, that's better than buying dozens of $10 air mattresses—but most consumers (and manufacturers) don't look at things that way.

There are good, sturdy air mattresses on the market, but you have to search for them. Those designed for backpackers feature separate air tubes, so that even with one or two punctures, they will still support your body off the ground. These are light mattresses that fold down into tiny packages, great for extended trips. At the other end of the scale are the old-fashioned canvas air mattresses, which are big and heavy but quite durable. Campmor offers both a single and a double mattress, both quite rugged. Couples who like to sleep close together and who camp out often enjoy the comfort the double mattress offers, and it isn't all that much heavier than two separate, flimsier mattresses.

Purely by accident, the IK market has produced what must be the world's toughest air mattress. Manufactured by Riken Inflatables, this mattress was originally designed as an inflatable floor for their IK line. The mattress is made of the same 25 percent Hypalon used in the construction of the Riken commercial rafts, so you know that no little sticks are going to puncture this baby. If the Riken mattress has a drawback, it is its availability; it is sold separately from the Riken IK and usually only to dealers. If you want one, you can try contacting Riken, or a Riken dealer might be willing to order one for you. Riken makes a short mattress that fits its K-1 and a longer one for its K-2; both are wonderful sleeping pads. The company also makes a great inflatable seat for IKs that doubles as an extension for the short air mattress, so your legs won't hang off the end.

Should you happen to own a Riken IK that came with a separate air mattress as a floor, or if you own another IK model that also has the removable floor feature, then there's no need to bother with carrying a second air mattress for sleeping. When you reach camp, remove the air mattress floor from the IK and prop it up to dry before bedtime. (You may have to deflate the IK tubes a little so that the mattress can be wiggled loose more easily.) You'll want to let some air out of the mattress, so that it's comfortable for sleeping. As with any air mattress, inflate it until it's just firm enough to support your weight. In the morning, put the mattress back into your boat, and you're ready to paddle.

Protect your air mattress from punctures by packing it into a nylon stuff sack or other protective container, and never place the mattress directly on the ground; use it in tents or on a sheet of plastic. Small holes in the body of the mattress can be repaired with the patch kit sold with the air mattresses or with duct tape. Seam failures, though, are difficult to fix and may signal the end of your inflatable bed. (In the event of a mattress failure, your IK may suffice as an emergency bed cushion.)

Air mattresses may be inflated by mouth, but using your IK pump is faster and easier. Because these pumps force air at a greater volume, you'll need to be careful not to overinflate the air mattress. A cheap mattress can burst, and most mattresses feel better if they're a little squishy anyway. You may have a problem fitting the big nozzle on the pump to the small valve on a typical air mattress. Inventive IK paddlers install Roberts valves with one-inch openings on their air mattresses, to match their heavy-duty foot pumps.

Some air mattresses come with built-in pillows, others are flat. If you need a separate pillow to sleep, by all means take one along. After a full day of paddling, you deserve a good night's sleep. Best are small camp pillows made of the same synthetic fill as sleeping bags—you don't want a huge, bulky pillow that takes up half your dry bag. Separate inflatable pillows are also available, or you can use a cushion from the IK. If you're tough and want to go light, use an article of clothing, such as a sweater, folded to shape. Or bring along a pillow case to make a pillow out of your clothes. Camp pillows are usually covered with nylon fabric that is tough but tends to let your head slide around; you can solve this problem by using a standard pillow case for your camp pillow. For a warmer, more luxurious pillow, sew your own case from flannel or polar fleece.

Still considering a foam pad? Then choose a closed-cell foam, such as ensolite, that won't absorb moisture. Open-cell pads are far too bulky and turn into sponges around moisture. Closed-cell pads offer better insulation from the cold ground than do air mattresses, because the dead air trapped inside an air mattress never warms. However, unless you paddle in the winter, or in the far north, you may never benefit from this advantage.

Camp Furniture

Today's camping ethics preclude the building of camp furnishings to leave behind for the next occupants of your site. With more people-pressure on wilderness areas, practicing "no-trace" camping techniques is important to keep the wild areas wild. However, conscientious camping doesn't have to mean discomfort. In addition to your cozy tent or shelter, your warm sleeping bag, and your luxurious air mattress, other camp comforts can be brought along on an IK trip.

Most popular, especially on an extended trip, is some kind of chair. Sitting on hard ground without back support gets tiring. Now on the market are several kinds of clever, lightweight chairs that elevate camp comfort to a new level. But before you rush out and buy a chair, keep in mind the go-light camper's creed: make everything do double-duty! If your IK is the kind with a removable seat, use the seat for a camp chair. Both rigid foam seats and inflatable seats make fine chairs. Of course, you need to be careful with a vinyl seat—don't set it down directly on the ground without some protection from pointy twigs.

If your IK doesn't have a removable seat, you can always buy an inflatable seat meant for use in a boat and use it in camp instead. These little gems pack down tight and add little weight to your load, a worthwhile tradeoff for the comfort they provide.

Not all free-standing seats provide the back support that feels good after a day of paddling, but the soft foam chairs, like the Power Lounger, will because they utilize the weight of your seated lower body to give your back a rest. These cost $40 to $50 from hiker suppliers, and they pack easily: stow them flat on the floor of your IK under the dry bag. (Some paddlers even use these in their IKs, to increase back support.) Small chairs that fold or break down into small pieces operate more like conventional chairs, but the metal pieces add both weight and bulk to the final package. Don't carry any kind of chair that has protruding metal edges unless there is plenty of padding to protect your IK.

Folding cots keep getting smaller, but so far, they just aren't practical for IK use, unless you have a supply raft accompanying your trip. The same goes for most camp tables, although the Roll-A-Table is compact enough to fit in some IKs, particularly the K-2s. It provides a great work surface for operating camp stoves, and for food preparation and equipment repair. Or try using the bottom of an IK for spreading out a lunch, although this isn't recommended as a cooking surface or for slicing vegetables, and you do have to be careful not to leave the IK in the hot sun.

Miscellaneous Items

On longer excursions, especially when the only available water is cold, a Solar Shower will be appreciated by all. This is a bag made with clear plastic on the top side and black plastic on the bottom. Operation is simple—all you need is a sunny day. Fill the bag with river water and place in the hot sun (in sand or on a rock is good) for several hours. Water inside the bag quickly warms to an agreeable shower temperature. When ready, hang the bag overhead from a tree limb, unclip the hose, and enjoy a warm shower! Solar Showers come in a personal size, a 2.5-gallon size great for couples, and a 5-gallon size that will clean up to a half-dozen people, depending on how much water each individual requires. The bag and hose rolls down to a tiny bundle and weighs just a few ounces.

For paddlers, the most wonderful feeling in the world is dry socks and shoes after a full day of wet feet. You'll want to be sure to pack along a pair of camp shoes. If you're just going to hang around on the beach, thongs are OK, but if you want to do some hiking, walking or running shoes will provide some ankle support for casual off-river exploration. Lugging hiking boots along may be difficult, because most are too heavy and bulky, although a pair of lightweight boots may prove useful.

Many items sold for backpacking work well for IK paddlers, too. Mini flashlights and candle lanterns provide plenty of light with minimum weight and bother. Also remember the personal comfort items. Nylon bags for toiletries keep the biodegradable soap and teeth-cleaning aparatus handy. Chapstick and hand lotion help increase your comfort level, especially in desert country. Nail clippers take up little space and are great for trimming the inevitable broken nails and hangnails. Don't forget a roll of toilet paper. Some like to take along a box of pre-moistened towelettes to freshen up with if the weather isn't conducive to swimming. Also, these are useful should someone come down with diarrhea, as they help prevent irritation of sensitive tissues caused by frequent wiping. Be sure to pack the used towelettes out or burn them in a hot fire; they don't biodegrade very well.

Small plastic trowels available from backpacker suppliers are great for digging personal latrines or scooping sand into a firepan. A small pack is useful for carrying your stuff during off-river hikes. Also useful, in addition to your PFD knife, is a Swiss Army knife or Leatherman tool; besides a cutting blade, these provide other tools, such as can openers, saw blades, and pliers.

FOR WOMEN ONLY

There are occasions when a man's anatomy seems better designed for the outdoors, such as when you're wearing a one-piece wetsuit and nothing underneath, and there are no trees, and you have to go, *now*! However, there is a solution. Currently available are little plastic funnels that allow women to urinate standing up. Once you become comfortable with their use, you will be amazed at the increased freedom and peace of mind you gain. One model even comes with heavy-duty plastic bags, so you can relieve yourself without being obvious—great for those long drives to the put-in that invariably have no restrooms and no trees! Brand names are SaniFem, Pocket Restroom, and Lady J; they are available from camping outfitters.

In the field, it's often easier to urinate at the edge of the river so you can wash with river water afterwards. This eliminates the continual need for toilet paper, while keeping you clean. (If you are wearing nylon running shorts, simply pull the crotch part to one side while you go—it's easier than undressing.) Using toilet paper is a nuisance in the unspoiled places, because it's ugly if tossed away, yet few are comfortable with the idea of bringing their used paper back to camp for burning or disposing in the garbage bag. If you prefer to use paper, stash it in a freezer-style (heavier-duty) Zip-Loc baggie—very secure. Carrying out or burning is also recommended for all feminine hygiene products, because they take a long time to decompose. Never leave these behind, even buried. By the way, tampons work better when you are wearing a rubber wetsuit or nylon shorts and being splashed by spray. Stick-on pads are good only in camp.

PROTECTING THE FRAGILE RIVER ENVIRONMENT

When you float a pristine waterway, you assume a responsibility to do everything you can to make sure it remains unspoiled. With a little care, your wilderness camp can be enjoyed without harming the environment. Start with the obvious: before you depart from a landing site, make certain not a speck of trash remains behind. This includes such things as cigarette butts, orange peels, twist-ties from bread wrappers, and other often-overlooked items. Don't leave any food scraps behind, using the rationale that "something" will eat it. Leaving food scraps behind, even buried scraps, attracts nuisances like yellow jackets and ants to the site. If you carried it in, carry it out! Feeding wild animals is bad for them, anyway—it teaches them to be beggars, and lessens their fear of humans, creating trouble for the next folks who camp.

A major source of pollution along well-used rivers is human waste. Unfortunately, no one has yet invented a solar restroom. If your trip is raft-supported, carrying a Porta-Potty helps protect the fragile river environment from human waste. Many popular rivers require boaters to take along some kind of system for carrying human waste down the river with them to prevent contamination of heavily used campsites. This requirement can be difficult on an all-IK trip. The only feasible solution is to carry a small container (an ammo can and seat, a plastic bucket with a snap-on lid, or a folding camp potty) and heavy plastic bags. Line the can with a bag and deposit wastes directly into the bag (solid wastes only—urinate in a spot well away from camp, or directly into the river, if it has sufficient flow to disperse the urine quickly). Sprinkle lime into the bag after each use. When breaking camp, close and tie the bag, place inside another bag for security, and pack inside the ammo can.

Some rivers, such as Oregon's Rogue, have outhouses located in popular camps. Others remain undeveloped—and pristine. If you don't have a waste disposal method, carry a plastic trowel. Choose a toilet site carefully, well away from any water source or campsite, and in dirt, not sand. Dig a cat hole about six inches deep. Fill in the hole after use. Don't bury toilet paper; carry it back to camp and burn it or place it into the garbage.

Campfires have always been a traditional part of camping, yet their impact on a fragile site can be devastating. Most people assume that only fires burning out of control are bad for the environment, but any fire built on a pristine beach ruins that site. Rocks blackened

This is what it's all about—getting into the wilderness. These paddlers are enjoying a quiet portion of the Rogue River canyon in Oregon.

by fire and ugly, half-burned logs can linger for years, until the river washes them away . . . down to the next beach. Build a campfire for warmth and cheer only, and do your cooking on a stove. Stoves offer steadier, more reliable heat, don't blacken pots, don't require constant attention, and they don't strip the site of vegetation.

Always build your fire in a container designed for this purpose, usually a metal fire pan. Something like a hubcap will work for a small fire, but on some rivers, fire pans with four-inch sides are mandatory. Also available is a product called the Fire Blanket, an asbestos-type blanket that qualifies as a fire pan container on most rivers with fire restrictions. The blanket easily folds or rolls into a small bundle suitable for packing into an IK. Besides keeping a fire from spreading, fire pans keep the burning materials off the beach. By containing ashes and charcoal, you can remove all evidence of your fire and carry it down the river with you. To use the fire pan, place a layer of sand or dirt in the bottom to prevent warping from the high heat. Keep your fire small, and avoid using large pieces of wood, so the fire will burn down clean, without leaving behind messy lumps of charcoal. Use only driftwood for your fire; it burns hotter and cleaner than other woods. (If campsites are short on wood, boaters can collect some during the day as they float, rather than strip each campsite bare of all sticks. This only works, though, when you have a support boat to carry the wood.) Let the fire burn down as far as possible and don't make a new one in the morning if you can avoid it. When the fire has cooled, store the refuse from the fire in an ammo can or rip-proof bag; use this as a base for the next fire. The fire pan is portable, so be careful when walking around in bare feet after the fire has been moved or put away—sand underneath the fire site stays scorching hot for hours and you can get a bad burn.

Never build a fire ring with rocks. If you come across someone else's fire ring built in a pristine area, take it apart and throw the rocks into the river. Scatter any remaining wood before you leave so that the site appears natural.

When bathing and washing dishes, use only biodegradable soap, available from any camp supply store. Strain kitchen waste water to remove food particles and pack this out as garbage; dump the waste water well above the river's high-water mark, away from camp. Frequent swimming reduces the need to bathe. The less soap you use, the better. Remember that even biodegradable soaps need time to break down after use. If you're lucky enough to encounter natural hot springs along the river, resist the urge to jump in with your soap; without a current to carry the suds away, they'll just sit there. Most hot springs have minerals in them that act as natural cleansing agents. If you must soap down, do it away from the spring, and have someone pour containers of hot water on you to wash off.

Building pools at wilderness hot springs sites is discouraged by both the Forest Service and the Bureau of Land Management; such pools usually wash out anyway. With a tarp and a paddle or two, you can make an excellent short-term hot tub. Position the tarp on the bottom of the pool site to form a floor and sides of a pool, then use rocks and paddles to hold the tarp in place. When the tarp fills with hot water, climb in and enjoy. The tarp eliminates most of the annoying scum that grows in hot springs, giving you a clean surface to sit on and a fresh pool of hot water to sit in. When you've finished soaking, remove the paddles and let the water drain out, then retrieve the tarp.

RIVER ETIQUETTE

Whitewater paddling is soaring in popularity. Sometimes it seems like everyone is on the river at the same time. While an IK offers you the freedom to escape the crowds, on occasion you'll find yourself sharing the river with others. Enhance everyone's river experience by exercising common courtesy.

Camping is usually first-come, first-served, except where all camps are reserved, in areas like Idaho's Middle Fork of the Salmon River. Respect other paddlers' camps—find your own site. If sites are full, ask another party if your group may join them, rather than just barging in. Camp as far away from the other group as possible, and don't abuse their hospitality by being loud all night. Whenever camps are close together, try to keep your group quiet and unobtrusive. Avoid walking into another group's camp. Likewise, find your own lunch sites, although it's acceptable to land at an occupied spot if that site is a common stopping place with something of interest to visit, such as a pioneer cabin, or a rapid to scout.

On the water, the downstream boat always has the right of way. Don't crowd others in a rapid; they may not be able to maneuver with your boat in their way. IKs need to keep clear of larger craft, especially big rafts, which require plenty of room to negotiate a river. Also, you don't want to be near when those heavy oars are swinging around—they're just about head-level with an IK paddler.

When you're about to pull away from a stopping point, check the river first to make sure another party isn't coming by. Don't paddle out into the middle of another group. Most knowledgeable river people are trying to keep their group together for safety's sake. Having your group in their midst is distracting. You may pass a slower group, if you accomplish this in quiet water, not in rapids, and don't crowd anyone.

Also be considerate of other river users, such as fishermen. Avoid paddling near or over their fishing lines. River users need each other to save rivers from dams and destruction; banding together is easier if each group respects the rights of the others.

It's helpful to know the "personality" of the river you're floating— not just where the rapids and camps are, but also what kind of people float the river. If you're floating a "splash-and-giggle" type of river, you can expect to find less-serious whitewater, more paddlers who like to party, and likely get involved in several spirited water fights. On the other hand, a river renowned for scenery and very technical whitewater may have no one on it except for a few serious, quiet paddlers who likely won't welcome a group of splash-and-gigglers in their midst. Respect the rights of other paddlers to enjoy the kind of river they came to experience.

Paddlers need to be aware of land ownership along the waterways they float. Even along a public river, there may be private property; abide by no trespassing signs, and don't litter private lands. Also avoid intruding on the privacy of landowners who live along a waterway, except if you have a real emergency. Those folks live there because they want to get away from it all, not to entertain every boater who happens by.

A lot of paddlers like to get back to nature, especially at riverbank hot springs, by taking off clothes. The freedom to skinny-dip is one of the great joys of wilderness paddling adventure for many people; however, for some, nudity can be offensive. If your group is in an isolated area, frolic freely. In a more heavily traveled area, be discreet—skinny-dip after dark.

PACKING

Efficient packing begins with lists. In the Appendix, you'll find lists of recommended gear for both day trips and overnighters. Not everything you might need or want is on these lists; they're just a starting place. After several trips, you'll have the experience to develop your own equipment lists. Going through items on a checklist is a sure way to be certain nothing vital gets forgotten; a trip can be ruined if someone shows up for a river trip without a life jacket, or if you get into camp and discover nobody remembered to bring matches.

The simplest—and most secure—way to pack is to carry one large dry bag in the stern compartment of your IK. This paddler has lots of room left over for more gear.

How gear fits into an IK depends on the individual boat. In general, you want to put as much gear as possible into one large dry bag. That one bag will hold much more than several smaller ones, and there is only one seal to worry about. It's easier to secure just one bag to the boat, too. If you have too much stuff to fit into one bag, perhaps you're trying to take too much. Sort through everything and reconsider each item: do you really need three pairs of underwear for a weekend trip?

The drawback to the one-bag system is finding a certain item you want. See-through bags are available, but most aren't as sturdy as opaque ones. Try to pack with unloading in mind; place camp items towards the bottom, warm clothing or rain gear you might want during the day towards the top. A supply boat can carry a "day bag" where paddlers can stow clothing and other items they might need before camp. On an IK, a small waterproof bag or fanny pack can be strapped on the boat to hold things you'll need during the day, like a camera (sealed in a waterproof container), sun lotion, gloves, and so forth. Keep a water container handy so you can drink during the day

Bulky gear such as fishing equipment or camera boxes will have to fit on last, after the essentials are loaded. When you load the IK for the first time, or if you are carrying different items, test the load at home first to make sure everything you want to take is going to fit. It's frustrating to get out to the river and discover that half your gear won't fit into the boat, or that you left an important item behind that would have fit, after all. Try different positions for your load without strapping things down, until you have a load that looks well balanced and secure.

To load an IK properly, keep the heavy items low and in the back of the boat. With most items in one large bag, this is easier. Keep in mind that your large bag packs vertically, but will rest horizontally in the IK. Try to pack soft things, like clothes, on what will be the top side of the bag. This acts as a cushion over the hard objects, which could injure a paddler during a flip. In a smaller IK, you may have trouble fitting the bag into the stern compartment between the tubes or underneath a stern spray shield. The tighter the bag fits, the less likely it is to pop loose.

If space appears tight after the big-bag essentials are packed, use creativity to stow the rest of what you want to take. Remember you'll be sitting in the front, so don't toss too many extra things in there. Under the bow spray shield, there's usually a little room to pack a water jug or two, as long as your feet won't be crowded. If you have no integral thwart under the seat, there may be enough room between the front and back parts of the seat to stash a tiny bag or something relatively rugged and waterproof, like canned drinks.

Before you tie the load and head down the river, test-paddle your load to make sure it's well balanced and not too heavy. If the load doesn't feel right, paddle back to shore and rearrange things, then try again. Have another paddler check the water line of your IK as you float. The IK tubes shouldn't be submerged below their middle point. Before you hit whitewater, you want your load to be balanced and secure.

Most boaters prefer straps to ropes for securing loads. With straps, you don't have to know any fancy knots. And they're easy to unfasten. In addition, straps cinch down tighter than ropes, with less effort. Always strap or tie down *everything* when you paddle an IK! Those side tubes are low to the water, and a loose item can easily tumble overboard, even on flat water. You'd be surprised how quickly things sink. And having gear fly loose in whitewater is both distracting and dangerous.

Some boaters feel, however, that tying gear down presents an entanglement hazard worse than the problem of lost gear. They prefer to leave everything loose in their boat. This may work if you have a solid backup to retrieve all your lost gear after it dumps out, but a properly secured load shouldn't entangle a boater. Giant rafts with enormous loads have flipped without entangling their passengers. Certainly, on a real wilderness expedition, you don't want to risk losing all your gear; the risk of spending a night out without your sleeping bag outweighs the risk of becoming entangled in the tie-down strap. Carrying a good river knife greatly reduces the hazard of entanglement.

When you strap down that load for the final time, make certain everything is secured tight. Use D-rings whenever possible to secure the load, so the straps won't slip in rough waters. If you have a lace-in floor, you might thread your straps through the gaps between floor and tube. On easy waters, you may be able to get away with strapping your load around the outside of the IK, but don't trust this in anything more than mild whitewater. Strap from side to side, not from side to end, when you can—this makes for a stronger tie-down. Be sure the straps go through something on the big bag (through grommets, D-rings, or straps on the bag) in addition to securing on two sides of the IK. Don't leave loose ends of the straps dangling; coil them and tuck them away, or better, use straps that are just long enough to accomplish the chore.

CAMP PROCEDURES

Prime campsites abound along most waterways. Rather than relying on chance to find a good site, some pre-trip research will help you decide when and where to stop for the day. You should know about how many miles you need to float each day, and have some idea of where you'll be in late afternoon, when you're ready to stop for the day. If the river is well known, there will be established camps listed and described in various guidebooks. Otherwise, you're pretty much on your own.

A suitable campsite should have a good landing spot for boats (such as a low beach) and flat space for beds. In hot weather, shade is essential; during stormy weather, look for a sheltered spot. You may find trees or bushes, caves or rock overhangs, or abandoned buildings to protect you from the elements. Natural resources—like a spring that supplies fresh drinking water or a pile of driftwood from last year's flood that will fuel your fire—are more of a bonus than a necessity. And you shouldn't count on finding drinkable water at very many campsites. Rather, fill your water containers at every opportunity.

Obviously, some spots offer less-than-ideal camping conditions. But the right equipment can sometimes overcome the drawbacks to an otherwise good site. For instance, a lumpy gravel bar may look uninviting to sleep on, but a reliable four-inch-thick air mattress will make those fist-sized boulders feel like a Sealy Posturepedic. And, with a good tent, you can get by without additional shelter during a storm.

Look for less-than-obvious drawbacks as well; these can make for a miserable night. A swampy area near camp may usher in a horde of mosquitoes at twilight. You need to be aware of special problems associated with the area, too, such as whether you're likely to come across chiggers in that soft, grassy spot, or whether the river might rise during the night and flood your camp.

Sandy beaches are clean, and feel wonderful underfoot, but don't forget that those little grains eventually find their way into *everything*. Beaches and gravel bars are the best choices for low-impact camping, because the river will eventually wash away all evidence of your visit, including footprints. Because they're scoured by the river on a regular basis, most beaches and gravel bars offer immaculate campsites.

When choosing a campsite, consider off-river activities. Keep an eye out for places to hike, or perhaps an interesting landmark to photograph in different lighting situations as the sun moves across the sky. A likely fishing hole, a good place to swim, or a few flecks of "color" for the gold-panning enthusiast may be more important to some paddlers than a great spot to tie up the boats.

After deciding on a camp, secure the boats. Because IKs are so light, they are especially vulnerable to blowing away in a wind or being washed down the river. As long as they're still loaded, IKs are fairly safe from the wind, but the moment those big bags are removed, it doesn't take much breeze to blow the boat back into the river and downstream. The quickest way to secure a fleet of IKs is to run a line through all the bow D-rings, then tie the ends of the rope to something solid, like a tree or a big rock. IKs can also be tied or clipped individually onto a line with a carabiner (useful if someone wants to paddle across to the other side for hiking or fishing) or strapped to an anchor. To tie boats, use a good, substantial knot such as the bowline, a knot that won't accidentally come undone, yet will be easy to untie. Or use a strong nylon strap with a reliable cam buckle to secure your IKs.

If the weather is quite warm, don't leave a fully inflated IK pulled up on land, because the increasing air pressure inside the air chamber could rupture a seam. On hot afternoons, leave the IKs tied up *floating in the water*, so they'll stay cooler. Check the air chambers frequently; if the tubes seem too tight, vent all chambers to prevent damage. (You will have to top off the IKs in the morning, but that's easier than dealing with a blown baffle.)

Once the boats are taken care of, the next step is selecting sleeping sites. Darkness can settle quickly in a deep canyon, so it's best to get shelters up and meals cooked early.

DEALING WITH NATURE'S DOWN SIDE

The risks involved in wilderness travel are part of the challenge of paddle adventure. A few sensible precautions, can minimize the risk of injury or illness during your trip. Be careful while on shore—keep in mind that most "river accidents" occur on or near land. Paddlers slip on slime-coated river rocks while wading the IK to shore, or take a tumble hiking to a scenic overlook. After successfully negotiating whitewater, paddlers can become careless on shore, believing themselves safe.

Hike with caution, especially around cliffs, loose rock, or muddy slopes. In snake country, watch where you put your feet and hands, and avoid tall grass. Snakes seem especially fond of tall grasses along the river that offer both shade from the hot sun and easy access to their prey. Take heavy footsteps to send out warning vibrations (snakes would much rather flee than fight), and poke a stick or paddle into tall grass before you commit your feet. If someone is bitten by a poisonous snake, get help immediately. Keep the victim calm, and elevate the bite area above the heart. Medical authorities can't agree on the effectiveness of a snakebite kit, but if you are far from civilization, cut-and-suck may be your only option, unless you carry an antivenom injection kit.

Besides snakes, grass along river banks can also harbor ticks, which can carry nasty diseases like Rocky Mountain Spotted Fever or Lyme Disease. To thwart ticks, spray insect repellent on body and clothing before hiking; wear long-sleeved shirts and long pants; tuck pant legs into socks or boots; and, in tick country, inspect for ticks immediately after hikes and each night—before you get into your tent. Ticks often take their time deciding on what part of your anatomy they want to bite; if you find them before they're attached, remove them with a flick of the finger.

If a tick becomes imbedded in your skin, it should be removed immediately (the sooner you get the tick out, the lower your risk of contracting an illness from it). Sometimes ticks will release their hold if you smother them with alcohol, oil of turpentine, Vaseline, or some other slimy substance. Or, light a match, blow it out, and apply to the tick's rear end—carefully. Probably the most reliable method of removing a tick is to grasp it with tweezers (or a special tick-removal tool available from mail-order camping equipment suppliers) and gently *unscrew* it. Be certain to remove the entire tick, and not just its body. If you are in known Lyme tick country, save the tick and have it examined for signs of the disease. See a doctor immediately if you have suspicious symptoms—a rash (especially in a circular pattern), fever, joint pains—because the disease can be treated.

Other bugs can pose problems for paddlers, as well. Bees and their stinging cousins may be attracted to the bright colors of PFDs, but generally don't sting unless you panic and start swatting. Persons known to be allergic to bee stings must carry a sting kit and know how to inject themselves with it; carrying such a kit on a long wilderness trip is a good idea even if no one is known to be allergic. Set up camp away from areas infested with yellow jackets. (In well-used campsites, they are often attracted to food scraps.) Some spiders and scorpions can inflict painful wounds, so use caution when poking around rocks or old buildings.

Mosquitoes are more of a nuisance than a real hazard, except in the far north, where swarms could make your paddle trip miserable. In such cases, wear head nets and special mesh garments soaked with repellent. Repellents, special clothing, and tent netting also help against black flies. For minor bug problems, try burning mosquito coils or building a smoky fire.

Unfortunately, like mosquitoes, the contact-poison plants also favor certain river environments. Poison oak is particularly widespread, even along beautiful wilderness streams like the Rogue River. Poison ivy and poison sumac may be encountered as well. Learn what these devilish plants look like and avoid touching them. The sap coming into contact with your skin causes the intense itching and blisters. A few unlucky folks react very strongly to the poison and might even have to be evacuated if a severe case is contracted. Carrying special soap to wash the skin after contact and the preventative lotion that is applied to sensitive skin before exposure is worthwhile for anyone in this category. Be especially careful not to burn the foliage of a contact-poison plant, or use the branches of these plants for marshmallow roasters—the results are unpleasant. To counter itching and swelling, apply soothing dressings (using cold water, baking soda and water, or calamine lotion) and take Benedryl antihistimine pills. Allergic persons should ask their physicians about a stronger remedy, such as cortisone.

Many campers worry about bears. If you are in black bear territory, your personal safety isn't seriously threatened, but your food and equipment may be trashed if left unprotected. The grizzly bear is much bigger, more aggressive, and considerably less predictable than its smaller relative. In grizzly country—limited to parts of the Rockies around Yellowstone, and north to Alaska—additional precautions are a good idea.

In any area where bears pose a problem, never take food into your tent. Also, be sure to wash well after food preparation, and sleep away from the kitchen area. Suspend food supplies from a tree, if possible. Never leave food inside an IK—a bear could rip your boat apart. Freeze-dried foods, in sealed pouches, don't have much odor and won't attract bears to your camp the way things like fresh meat will. When you break camp in bear country, clean the site and carry all the garbage out, so other campers won't have to deal with bears coming around in the middle of the night uprooting your buried cans.

When traveling through grizzly country on foot, make some noise so you don't surprise a bear. Hang a bell on your belt loop, carry a can with pebbles, or whistle while you walk. Many campers carry something to equalize a confrontation with a grizzly, such as a flare that, when set off, might frighten away even a bear not afraid of people. Carrying a firearm is a precaution many paddlers who travel the wild areas of the north woods prefer—but be sure to pick a weapon capable of disabling a grizzly, such as a shotgun with rifle slugs. If you have a smaller firearm, don't even bother to fire at the bear—although shooting into the air might produce sufficient noise to make a grizzly reconsider. (A firearm also serves as an emergency signaling device and a means of procuring meals in survival situations, especially in remote areas.)

While bears are an obvious danger, even a small animal can injure you. Of course, an enjoyable part of being outdoors is viewing and photographing wild animals, but you should never try to approach any wild animal, no matter how cute. Animal mothers will bite to protect their young. An animal that appears tame may in fact have rabies. That cuddly bunny could be carrying bubonic plague fleas. Also, don't feed the animals—this makes moochers out of wild creatures and lessens their fear of humans, causing problems for the next paddlers.

While animals are seldom a problem in wilder areas where they avoid humans, in more developed sites, many have learned that campers mean free food. Skunks, in particular, may pose a hazard to non-tenters, because they fear no one. Generally skunks will leave you alone unless you interfere with them—so give them lots of room if you encounter them.

WEATHERING STORMS

Storms in the backcountry can be either miserable or exciting experiences, depending on how well prepared you are. If you can, get a reliable weather forecast before you launch so you know what to expect. Always go rigged for rain, even on a desert trip; and even during a heat wave, carrying some extra warm clothing is a sensible precaution.

If a thunderstorm threatens nearby while you are paddling, get off the water and take cover. Look for a group of smaller trees, rather than one tall tree, which could act like a lightning rod.

Heavy rains or strong winds demand good shelter, but few tarps can stand up to them. In a powerful storm, improvise shelter: drape your tarp over a table or boulder, and anchor the ends with rocks if tying to trees won't work. Stake your tent down securely and put heavy gear inside it, so it won't blow away. Secure IKs and PFDs, and strap down paddles. Stow loose gear in river bags, which can be tied down. Stay off beaches, where loose sand will be blown around with great force.

If a driving rain begins while you're on the river, you must decide whether to keep going or to stop and seek shelter. If your party is well dressed and in good shape, you may elect to keep paddling. If someone is cold and tired, stopping will be necessary. Keep an eye on weather that threatens off in the distance; you may be able to beat a storm to camp and get everything ready before the bottom falls out. Rigging tents and cooking are much easier if done before the storm hits, not in the thick of it.

Look for natural shelter along the river. Caves, although not common, offer excellent protection, besides being fun to stay inside. Rock shelters or a row of thick brush will block strong one-directional winds. Large, leafy trees may have dry spots underneath, close to the trunk. In a pinch, you might camp under a bridge or a picnic table, if available. And don't forget the IK. Although not as comfortable as sleeping under a big canoe, IKs do function adequately as emergency shelters.

Unless a cooperative sun appears to dry your tents, it's best to pack the wet parts inside heavy-duty garbage bags, separating them from other things, then dry them out later. If things get really wet, a fire can help in the drying process, but be careful; tents are easily damaged by fire. At all costs, keep the sleeping bag dry.

THE FIRST AID KIT

For a short trip, one of the compact first aid kits with assorted Band-aids and painkillers (such as aspirin, Tylenol, Motrin) will suffice. But for a more extensive expedition, you'll need a well-stocked first aid kit. You can buy such a kit from camping supply stores, or put together your own. Discuss your medical needs with your family physician, especially if prescription drugs are necessary.

Knowledge is the crucial component of any good first aid kit.

Paddlers should be well versed in basic first aid and CPR. Also, carry a good book on backcountry medicine (*Medicine for Mountaineering* is popular, although some of the information is irrelevant for boaters). Of course, the exact contents of the first aid kit will vary, depending on the needs of individual paddlers and the length of the trip.

Unless you are a physician or know one well, acquiring prescription drugs for your first aid kit can be difficult. For most situations, however, over-the-counter medications will work as well, and may be safer (less risk of an allergic reaction, for instance). The most useful prescription drug for backcountry medicine is acetaminophen with codeine (Tylenol-codeine); it's far safer than more potent painkillers and allows the victim to function with an injury or be evacuated. The codeine also helps fight diarrhea. Usually, doctors are willing to prescribe small amounts of Tylenol-codeine for emergency first aid use. These tablets may be available over-the-counter in other countries, particularly Canada. Ibuprofen, aspirin, and plain acetaminophen all help fight pain and inflammation from injury. Responses to these medications vary, so carrying all three is a good idea.

Lomotil is another useful prescription drug, one that shuts down diarrhea quickly. You should always have something along for treating diarrhea, because it's miserable on a wilderness trip. Also, a long bout with diarrhea can leave a victim seriously dehydrated. A good nonprescription diarrhea medication is Imodium. Pepto-Bismol works for minor cases, too. Choose pills rather than liquids; they weigh less and there's no risk of spillage.

For wounds, carry an assortment of bandages. Butterfly-type closures are useful for closing gaping wounds. Include soap for cleansing wounds and antibiotic ointment to prevent infection. Large gauze pads should be included for extensive wounds. Adhesive tape will attach pads and provide protection to blister-sensitive palms. Use folding scissors for cutting tape and pads. You may want to carry a broad-spectrum antibiotic tablet, available only by prescription; if you do, be careful when dispensing: some people have nasty allergic reactions to antibiotics. Getting a tetanus shot or booster before the trip may be advisable, too.

Another good drug to carry is Diphenhydramine (trade name Benedryl) in 25-milligram doses. Once available by prescription only, this powerful antihistimine has many uses: as an allergy suppressant for hay fever, a decongestant for cold sufferers, a great itch reliever for insect bites or poison oak, and as a sedative for restless nights. This last use is sometimes the drug's main drawback: it makes you sleepy. To suppress allergic reactions without drowsiness, the prescription drug Seldane (sometimes available over-the-counter in other countries) is effective.

For bone, joint, and muscle injuries, include an elastic bandage, triangular bandage, a cold pack (in case ice or cold river water is not available to combat swelling), and a splint (sometimes improvised using a paddle blade, the foam floor from an IK, sticks, etc.) to immobilize suspected fractures.

Other items you may find useful include: hydrocortisone cream and calamine lotion (for topical treatment of poison oak), burn gel packet (for serious burns), Solarcaine (for sunburn), Block-out or zinc oxide (to shield skin against further sun exposure, especially the face), snakebite/antivenom kit, bee-sting kit, dental emergency kit, activated charcoal tablets (for treating poisonings), and antacids.

Everything will need to be packaged in a waterproof container. Small Zip-Loc baggies located on top of the load are handy for frequently used essentials (Band-aids, aspirin or other painkiller, sun lotion). Small ammo cans or Pelican-style cases work for the first aid kit. Emergency items can be vacuum-sealed separately or together, to protect them from moisture. The small kits sold for backpackers aren't waterproof, nor are they sufficient for a real expedition.

HYPOTHERMIA

This dangerous lowering of the internal body temperature probably kills more outdoor enthusiasts than any other hazard. IK boaters are especially at risk because they paddle right in the waves, risking continual dousings of cold water. Also, the combination of paddling effort and cold can exhaust a paddler more quickly than just cold alone.

Hypothermia is easier to prevent than treat; and it's easier to treat in its early stages than later on. Use the buddy system to keep an eye on each other for early symptoms of hypothermia (irritability, unresponsiveness to questions, fatigue, shivers) and stop the entire group should someone start to feel very chilled, or fall overboard in cold water.

For mild cases, get the victim out of wet things and into dry, warm clothes. If the weather is at all windy or cold, shelter the victim—from the cold ground with a pad or PFD, from wind with a tent or space blanket. Give the victim plenty of hot liquids such as cider, and build a fire or wrap the victim in a blanket to provide additional warmth.

Don't delay; prompt action is important to prevent the victim from lapsing further into hypothermia. (Avoid alcohol—it worsens hypothermia.)

For more severe cases, such as a victim uncontrollably shivering after a dunking in cold water, strip the victim and place him or her inside a sleeping bag. Two warm people should also strip down and get inside the bag, one on each side of the victim. (You may have to use several sleeping bags, but seal off the wind and cold.) In cases of severe hypothermia, the victims lose the ability to rewarm themselves. They must have outside warmth applied quickly, or they could die. Sure, it's fun to joke about scheduling "hypothermia drills" for the above technique, but remember that hypothermia is no laughing matter—it's a potential killer.

7

THE IK CUPBOARD

The menu on an all-IK trip is somewhere between the extravagance of an outfitted raft excursion—often boasted of as a "float-and-bloat" trip, with steaks, beer, and almost anything else you could want—and the Spartan diet of the backpacker, heavily based on freeze-dried meals. What kind of food you pack into the IK depends on how long the trip will last, what the weather will be like, how much weight your IK can hold, and the personal preferences of the trip participants.

Meals can be planned and prepared individually, or for a group. Sharing the chore makes sense: if everyone can agree on a menu, then the meals can be cooked in communal pots, on group stoves, requiring less gear and stove fuel.

Unless you're headed out for a month-long trip, don't worry too much about eating a balanced diet. On most trips, you can eat pretty much what you would eat at home—with a few notable exceptions. Of course, you will want to take food that satisfies you and gives you lots of energy for paddling.

ICE CHESTS

The biggest problem for paddlers traveling independent of a support boat is refrigeration. Traditional ice chests are extremely bulky and impossible to consider for all but the largest IKs. One large IK can take a medium-sized cooler, provided the other paddlers help out by absorbing some of the extra load it displaces.

But now there are the new "soft" coolers, made of flexible fabric instead of rigid plastic. The beauty of these is that the cooler isn't taking up half the boat once it's empty—just squash it flat. They cost more than the traditional ice chests, but are worthwhile if you like to pack fresh foods. Look for a soft cooler that's built tough, and treat it kindly, because it won't take the abuse you're used to giving the hard plastic ice chests.

Even a good soft cooler won't hold a lot of food. If you take one or two soft coolers, plan your meals carefully so you use fresh foods as a treat, rather than a staple. Small amounts of meats can be used successfully in meals like stir-fry, shish kebabs, or rice dishes. To make meats last as long as possible, freeze them solid. A clever trick to extend them even longer is to freeze the already-frozen meat inside a block of ice, layer by layer. The meat will keep until the block of ice has almost entirely melted.

Inspect meats frequently to make sure they are staying cool; you don't want anyone to get food poisoning on the trip. Plan on using meats early in the trip. Fish, like salmon steak, and pork won't keep as long as beef and chicken. Wrap all meats, especially chicken, carefully so juices don't leak all over everything. Double-freezer bags of the Zip-Loc variety work great for this.

Less touchy in terms of refrigeration are cheeses, lunch meats, and vegetables. Some boaters place these items in plastic bags, which they carry in the bottom of their craft on the theory that the cold river water will keep them cool. And don't bother chilling canned drinks in the cooler—use a river dunk bag for this, otherwise the warm cans will eat away all of your ice.

GETTING BY WITHOUT REFRIGERATION

Most food items should be the kind that don't require chilling. Even with no refrigeration, you may expect to eat well on an IK trip. Canned foods are great if used in moderation (they're also heavy and bulky), and small cans of chicken or turkey, tuna fish, corned beef, deviled ham, and the like will keep you in protein for a long time. On the vegetable side, canned garbanzo beans can make a handy lunch spread (mix with peanut butter and season to taste) or use them in a salad. A can of mixed stir-fry vegetables will give you Chinese take-out food on the river.

You can even grow mung bean or alfalfa sprouts for fresh vegetables. Use a small plastic container with a screw-on lid for this. Cut out the top of the lid and glue in a circle of mesh, either heavy plastic or metal screen. For trips shorter than a week, start the sprouts at home several days before you leave. Sprinkle seeds into the bottom of the container, fill with water, and let sit overnight. In the morning, drain the water and rinse with fresh water. Rinse up to three times a day, making sure the seeds aren't left sitting in water. When the sprouts start to show a hint of green, they're ready to use. Alfalfa sprouts make a good substitute for lettuce in sandwiches and salads. Mung beans are used most often in Chinese dishes, but experiment freely; they take little cooking and are very mild-flavored.

If you like gourmet foods, try a place like Hickory Farms for excellent sausages, beef sticks, cheeses, and other goodies; most of these will keep a few days, sometimes longer, without refrigeration. Summer sausages, jerky, smoked salmon, and other meat treats are available in most supermarkets. Most hard cheeses keep reasonably well without ice; they need to be completely sealed in plastic or wax.

TIPS FOR FOOD PREPARATION

If you're really into expeditions, and like to do things for yourself, you might consider purchasing one of the fancy vacuum-seal appliances (known by the trade name Foodsaver). These gizmos suck all the air out of a heavy-duty plastic bag, and seal it tight. Anything can be sealed in the bags from blocks of cheese to socks you want to keep clean and dry. This allows you to buy in bulk, then package everything into smaller units, without waste due to spoilage. Contact with the air is what causes most foods to spoil; even meats packaged this way will keep longer in the freezer without risking freezer burn. It's also a great way to protect things like extra batteries from moisture. (Don't confuse the vacuum-type machine with the simpler, cheaper food sealing devices that don't create the full vacuum seal necessary to preserve foods.)

Use the vacuum sealer or Zip-Loc baggies in pre-trip packaging. This method works wonders for reducing food preparation chores on the river. For example, powdered beverage mixes can be measured and packaged into one-quart (or any volume you need) packets, ready to mix in a canteen. Measuring is much easier in your home kitchen than on a beach with the wind blowing. If you plan on doing any baking, mix the necessary dry ingredients into a bag beforehand. Later, on the river, you just add wet ingredients and stir. With a sturdy bag, you won't even need utensils and bowls—just add water, then close the bag and knead it until the ingredients are well mixed.

STOVES AND COOKING EQUIPMENT

While cooking over an open fire conjures up a romantic image of "real" camping, reality is quite different. Open fires blacken cooking pots, making a sooty mess that is difficult to clean outdoors. Temperatures over open fires vary wildly. Fires consume wood for fuel, which may be hard to find along some rivers. And for efficient cooking with pots, a grate is necessary, which adds to your boat's weight, besides being difficult to pack.

In short, cooking over an open fire is out of style for today's environmentally conscious paddlers. Stoves are much more efficient and far easier on the environment. Of course, you needn't give up all open-fire cooking—an occasional hot dog or marshmallow begs to be roasted over flames, and using hot coals to cook a meal in foil once in a while won't hurt anything, either.

Stoves suitable for IK trips are backpacker or other lightweight stoves that burn white gas, butane, propane, or alcohol (Sterno). The best fuels are white gas and propane, the main difference being whether you prefer carrying out disposable propane cylinders or refilling gasoline containers.

These stoves are single burners, great for cooking one-pot dishes, but obviously a two-course meal is difficult to manage. However, if a group of paddlers is sharing meals, it's worth considering a two-burner such as the popular models made by Coleman. These stoves are fairly small and lightweight, considering that they replace two smaller stoves. They are rugged, stand up to a lot of abuse, and are easy to operate even under the worst of conditions; they offer a more stable cooking surface and versatility (you can cook oatmeal and make coffee at the same time). A three-burner is also available, but is much larger and harder to pack; for a big group, first consider a pair of two-burners.

Cooking equipment can be simple or elaborate, depending on what you want to cook. One large pot, such as a stock pot from the local department store, will serve lots of people; or you can buy the small mess kits available from camping supply stores. Before you buy, check to make sure pots will fit on your stove—many large pots won't fit on small backpacker-style stoves. Remember that pots with lids heat more efficiently. Aluminum is a good material: lightweight and strong.

You'll need some kind of pot holder—a bandanna, at the least, or a good mitt. Some small pots come with their own. Don't forget a stirring spoon, a can opener, and any other utensils you may require to complete your meals.

FOODS FOR IK TRIPS

Pack along some staple foods that supply complex carbohydrates to fuel your body for a day of paddling. Good for this, and easy to fix on a camp stove, are grain products such as oatmeal, rice dishes (like Rice-A-Roni and Lipton Rice and Sauce Mixes), pasta, and pre-packaged boxes of macaroni and cheese. Potatoes can be baked by wrapping them in heavy-duty foil and placing them in the coals of a campfire. Other potato products are available in quick-to-fix packages, such as hash browns, au gratin, or sour cream and chive. Beans are a camp staple, but most take too long to cook. Canned pork and beans are popular and easy to prepare: just heat the whole can (remove label first). For mornings when you want to get on the river quickly, granola bars or instant cold cereals are both tasty and filling. If you have more time, concoct a satisfying breakfast of pancakes.

Fresh vegetables and fruits are bulky and can spoil, but they are wonderful on a camping trip. Carrots, celery, radishes, and similar vegetables keep fairly well if the weather isn't too hot, as do apples, pears, and oranges. Choose fruits that are a little underripe, and let them ripen on the trip. Use fully ripe fruit promptly or it will bruise. Oranges are popular because they are durable, and they provide both Vitamin C and a source of liquid.

Dried fruits, especially apricots, are great on paddle trips. They provide a good source of quick energy without resorting to candy. Many experienced wilderness trippers dry their own fruits. With a food dryer, you can enjoy exotics like cherry raisins, dried nectarine slices, dehydrated kiwis, or soft banana chips (far superior to the hard chips available commercially). Combine a food dehydrator with a vacuum sealer, and you can package piles of long-lasting goodies for future trips.

Nuts are another good energy food for paddling. A mix of nuts and dried fruits, perhaps with some M & Ms candy thrown in, makes a filling lunch or snack. Buy these as "trail mix" or "Gorp" (which reportedly stands for "good old raisins and peanuts"). Chocolate—either the pure kind or with nuts in it—is great (at least until it melts), as are yogurt-coated nuts. Salted nuts offer a good way to keep your body in shape during hot weather without resorting to salt tablets. Peanut butter is wonderful on float trips (the natural kind can survive without refrigeration for a few days, and the sugary kind provides a little extra energy boost). Unshelled peanuts, sunflower seeds, and pistachio nuts are poor choices, because the hulls make a real mess.

Freeze-dried foods have their advantages, especially for longer trips. Most are one-pot meals and require a minimum of fuss, a boon after you've paddled hard all day. The best ones don't require any cooking or dishes at all, other than a pot to boil water in. With these, you just pour the recommended amount of boiling water into the pouch, fold it down to keep the heat in, and wait the recommended time. Then eat directly from the pouch. Many different meals are available in freeze-dried form these days, so you will want to look them over and try a few at home to see if you like them.

Things you eat at home all the time, like bread, milk, and eggs, may be difficult to take down the river with you. Although bread tends to squash easily, if you choose the denser kinds like rye or whole wheat, it will keep reasonably well. Pack bread into a plastic container with a snap-on lid to prevent mashing. Many boaters prefer to use pita bread or tortillas for sandwiches, eliminating the bread problem. Milk is most often taken along in powdered form, to be mixed on the spot with water for dousing cereal or drinking straight. Powdered milk has come a long way from the horrible stuff they made you drink in summer camp. Both Milkman and Carnation make palatable powdered milks. Powdered eggs are another matter entirely; except for baking, nobody seems to use them these days. More common are freeze-dried eggs packaged as omelets, which taste better than the powdered ones ever did, anyway. However, for baking, powdered eggs or egg substitutes are useful. They can be pre-mixed into dry ingredients beforehand, eliminating the need for fresh eggs in brownies, cakes, and other goodies.

BEVERAGES

Especially on cold mornings, many campers like hot drinks. Some won't consider getting out of sleeping bags unless there's a pot of hot coffee on. Coffee can be instant or brewed, depending on how you like it. Cocoa and cider come in single-serve packets that mix instantly with hot water heated on the camp stove. If you are forced to boil river water for drinking, a packet of hot drink mix will make it more palatable. On cold evenings, a warm drink before bedtime helps keep you cozy during the night. Also, anytime the weather and water are cold, it's a good idea to have a thermos filled with hot water handy in case someone becomes chilled or gets dunked, because a hot liquid quickly administered will help ward off hypothermia. Hauling out the stove and finding a pot to heat water in, priming the stove, and waiting for water to boil all take time. Use instant-mix drinks with the hot water—even a packet of Jello mixed strong will deliver a quick sugar fix that warms the insides.

Many people like canned drinks on a river trip—both pop and beer—but they are bulky and difficult to carry on an all-IK trip. Some boaters rationalize carrying them on the grounds that cans take up no more room than does water, and taken along in moderation, they won't overload your IK. On trips with tougher whitewater, however, they're best left behind. A burlap bag or mesh dunk sack lets you keep them cool in the river, but don't drag this behind your IK like the rafters do; use it in camp.

Also good for float trips are powdered cold drink mixes, such as iced tea, lemonade, Kool-aid, Tang, and so forth. Select brands you enjoy at home. Sugar-free drink mixes with Nutrasweet flavor your drinking water with fewer calories, but more importantly, they take up considerably less volume in the kitchen supplies, a benefit on long expeditions, especially if you must drink treated water, which can have a strange taste.

Whatever your preference for drinks, be sure to drink enough liquids to avoid dehydration. Even in cold weather, keeping your body hydrated is important—you lose fluids paddling. Drink often, regardless of whether you feel thirsty or not, especially in hot, dry weather. While canned drinks are popular, remember to drink plenty of water straight; this replenishes your body's supply more quickly than sugary drinks.

THE WILDERNESS WATER PROBLEM

Another reason canned drinks are popular is the uncertainty of drinkable water on many trips. It seems absurd that while on a wilderness *float* trip, of all things, running out of water should be a major concern. However, due to contamination by a nasty microscopic pest known as *Giardia,* drinking directly from the river below you is risky. Even the most remote mountain stream isn't safe these days, as the Giardia cyst is spread by animals like beaver and cattle as well as by people.

The main river may also contain other contaminants, especially if it has human habitation or activity upstream. Side creeks are a little better, but springs bubbling directly out of solid rock or ground uncontaminated by animals are the only sure source of pure water.

By bringing water from home to use, and filling up only at springs, you can get by without having to use questionable water on a lot of trips. But if you plan on using river or stream water, pre-treatment is recommended to prevent illness. Getting sick on a long wilderness trip is no picnic. If you've been infected with Giardia, prescription drugs are necessary to recover. The symptoms are severe diarrhea and abdominal cramps.

The Giardia cyst is a tough little bug and is hard to destroy in the field. Even some city reservoirs have had treatment systems fail. Books on wilderness camping used to recommend halazone tablets or other chemicals, which may or may not kill the cysts. Boiling will, but it must be sustained for five to ten minutes. An easier and safer way is a water filtration system (such as the type made by Katadyn) which forces water through a ceramic filter. A very fine filter is required to screen out Giardia cysts; make sure your filtration system will do the job properly.

Carrying Water

Carrying several gallons of clean water increases your float trip options; specifically, you don't need to camp at a spring each night to restock. Carry at least a one-gallon jug on overnight trips, plus a smaller bottle for sipping during the day.

The easiest way to carry water on an all-IK trip is in plastic jugs. Recycle old milk, bleach, or orange juice jugs for this purpose. Of course, you must be careful to throughly rinse and air out a jug that once contained bleach. Milk jugs should be rinsed and aired promptly after emptying, as well, because the smell of sour milk lingers forever in plastic. (Use a few drops of vanilla extract, swished around inside, then rinsed out, to combat odors in plastic containers.) The three-quart orange juice jug is just the right size for stuffing into the bow of a K-1, and is easier to clean out than jugs that contained other liquids.

Smaller water containers, of plastic or metal, are available from camping supply stores. Because they're lighter in the hand, even when full, they're much easier to drink from. A small water bottle kept handy encourages frequent drinking and helps avoid dehydration. Sports squirt bottles and canteens are popular; refill these from bigger jugs or directly at safe springs.

KEEPING FOODS DRY AND INTACT

Nothing could be worse than arriving in camp and unpacking, only to discover you've lost half your food supply because something leaked. Careful packaging will help ensure dry foods stay dry until they're needed. For ultimate security, seal anything that can be harmed by water into Zip-Loc or vacuum-sealed bags. Be sure to squeeze out all the extra air in the Zip-Loc baggies before sealing, for a better seal and less bulk. The most secure place to pack food is inside the big bag. For efficiency, package meals in an orderly fashion, such as a day's meals inside one bag, and identify contents with a felt marker. On an expedition requiring large amounts of food, you may have to empty food out of its original packaging and repack into baggies, to cut down on unnecessary bulk.

When packing, don't forget to pack lunch items where they'll be readily accessible, yet dry and secure. You don't want to have to dig through a week's food supply for your lunch. Have knives and cutting boards handy, also.

Try to select food items with tough packaging, or repackage things so they will resist rough treatment. Plastic jars and squeeze bottles are much better in the field than glass containers. Backpacker suppliers sell special squeeze tubes for items such as jam. If you must take glass containers, seal them in double layers of Zip-Loc baggies for additional security against breakage. Broken bottles can puncture a dry bag or IK, and a broken container means you must throw away the food item that was inside.

FOOD SAFETY

Avoiding sickness assumes more importance on an expedition, because it's no fun to suffer through food poisoning on a long trip. Meats are the usual culprit—use them only if they stay fresh and cold. Discard any suspicious-looking food, and remember to cook chicken and pork until they're well done. Wash hands, knives, and cutting boards thoroughly after contact with any raw meat. Don't let raw chicken juices drip onto anything that won't be cooked, because chicken often carries salmonella. If you use mayonnaise or other spreads, buy the tiny jars and use them up, rather than rely on one large container for many days. Check package labels to see which foods require refrigeration—many do after they've been opened. Try to plan meals so that everyone has enough food and leftovers are minimal. If you have leftovers that can't be kept cold, put them into the trash.

Knives and cutting boards need to be washed and disinfected after each use. Sheath knives, popular with campers, can harbor bacteria in the sheath. Folding knives aren't much cleaner. The best choice for cutting food is a fillet knife that comes with its own plastic sheath. The sheath is easy to sterilize with boiling water or chlorine bleach and keeps the knife from poking holes into things. Get one with a stainless steel blade so it won't rust.

Each paddler should have his or her own personal eating utensils, including a cup, and take charge of washing them. This helps prevent the spread of disease, and makes cleanup easier. Store your utensils in a plastic bag with your name written on it, so you won't use the wrong set by accident. Heavy-duty plastic or stainless steel utensils are easy to clean and won't tarnish.

Don't use untreated water for brushing teeth or rinsing your drinking cup. For washing dishes, a three bucket system is recommended: hot soapy wash, warm rinse, and cold soak with a teaspoon of chlorine bleach added to several gallons of water. Carrying three buckets may be hard on an all-IK trip, but if everyone is using their own silverware, soaking in bleach will sterilize them sufficiently. (The chlorine bleach sterilizes the river water; unless you are camped at a spring, don't use drinking water for washing dishes or faces—use the river.)

LIVING OFF THE LAND

Drifting some rivers, you may be able to supplement food carried in with the fish you catch, or with edible wild plants. Along some ocean beaches, the range of native seafoods is generous: limpets, clams, oysters, mussels, sea urchins, shrimp, prawns, crab, and even lobster. Knowledge of edible wild plants and animals is a valuable survival skill for would-be wilderness paddlers, and an enjoyable hobby that can come in handy on a long trip where only freeze-dried foods are carried.

If nature offers an unexpected bounty of fresh huckleberries or trout, enjoy! However, it's best not to count on living off the land; fish can be uncooperative and plants scarce. Before you go nibbling leaves or berries, of course, you must know what you're doing. On the Owyhee River several years ago, a boater died after consuming deadly poisonous water hemlock root, which he misidentified as a wild parsnip. His companions who sampled the roots became ill from just a few small pieces.

Excellent resources are available for paddlers interested in learning about wild foods: dozens of good books, classes with field trips to identify and taste plants, even video tapes of edible and poisonous plants. Learn what poisonous plants (and the rare toxic animals) look like—know what to avoid.

Also consider the environment before you start plucking. Picking berries causes no harm, but digging up roots kills the entire plant. In fragile desert areas, plants are scarce and may take years to grow back, if they ever do. The best edible plants are what most people consider "weeds," so removing them won't be harmful, but be careful of eating an attractive wildflower—it might be a rare species.

GOING GOURMET

On a raft-supported trip, pull out all the stops. It's fun to try your hand at being an outdoor gourmet. River guides enjoy cooking all sorts of surprises outdoors for their guests, from Cornish game hens to fresh whipped cream for a hot apple pie.

Even without a support boat, paddlers can sit down to tasty baked goods for dinner. For outdoor baking, use a Dutch oven, a large pot with three legs on the bottom (to sit over coals) and a raised lip around the lid (to hold coals on top for even heat distribution). An aluminum Dutch oven is fairly lightweight and cooks almost as well as the traditional cast iron. A 12-inch model serves six to eight; a 10-inch will satisfy smaller groups.

For fuel, most chefs prefer charcoal briquets; they give out the steady, even heat necessary for good baking. Carrying a heavy, bulky bag of briquets can be tough on an all-IK trip, because it takes about two to three pounds for each baking session. Pack charcoal securely to keep it dry, and to keep the black soot from dusting everything else. Using match-light charcoal eliminates the need for separate lighter fluid.

Before using a Dutch oven, it's a good idea to spray it with non-stick coating, wipe some vegetable oil around the inside, or line it with foil. This will make your food pop out with minimal cleanup. Also, by using foil pouches, you can bake several batches in one

Dutch oven baking with charcoal briquets. Sourdough biscuit batter fermented and rose while boats floated down the river to camp.

oven—just exchange pouches when the first is done. If you're baking something that needs preheating, put coals on the lid while you ready the food. You will need tongs and a padded mitt to work with the coals and a pair of pliers to handle the hot lid. Position the hot coals so that about five to six are underneath the oven (away from the three legs) with enough on top to fully encircle the *outer* rim of the lid (about eighteen to twenty coals).

Generally, things cook in the Dutch oven in about the same length of time that they do at home. When the food is almost done, you will be able to smell it. Wait a few minutes after you first smell the food, then lift the lid and take a peek. If you're baking bread or a dessert, test it with a knife tip. When the food no longer sticks to the knife, it's ready.

Any prepared mix, like a box of fudge brownie mix, will bake up wonderfully in a Dutch oven. You can whip up cobblers and so forth from scratch, using biscuit mix as a base, or get creative and turn out pineapple upsidedown cake, muffins, or even bread. As a main course, lasagna is heavenly after a long day on the river. Layer cooked noodles, preheated spaghetti sauce, mozzarella, and Provolone or other cheese inside a foil pouch (it's messy!). Bake about ten minutes, or until the cheese melts.

Remember, if you're short on space, the Dutch oven also doubles as a stove pot for stews and other main courses. Some boaters saw the legs off, then use rocks or smashed aluminum pop cans to elevate the oven above the bottom coals.

For baking with less weight and bulk, there are several options: the "Bakepacker" type mini-oven, Coleman's folding stovetop oven, or homemade ovens (assembled from pie pans). Some inventive folks even do outdoor baking in a Chinese wok.

TAKING OUT THE TRASH

All your garbage must be carried out with you. Also, pick up any trash left by others—litter invites more litter. When packing trash, try to cut down on its bulk as much as possible. Many campers like to smash aluminum cans flat and store them separately for recycling. Regular tin cans should have top and bottom removed, then be flattened for disposal or recycling. Bend the lids in half and tuck them inside the flat can, to avoid sharp edges. Some boaters on long expeditions smash all glass containers (place glass inside a durable plastic bag first) to eliminate bulk.

Paper trash may be burned in the fire, but be sure to add each piece separately, so the trash will burn completely. Never try to burn cans, foil, or those empty freeze-dried food packets—they don't burn (but in bear country, burn these before packing them into the trash bag, to cut down on odor). Organic trash like orange peels may or may not burn completely; sift the fire for residue and take it out with you. Used toilet paper and feminine hygiene products should be burned or carried out—never leave these behind, even buried. Your fire residue is considered trash and must be packed out. You can re-use the ashes under the next fire, which helps reduce the bulky charcoal.

Before you leave any stopping spot, police the site thoroughly, checking for such annoying bits of trash as cigarette butts, plastic or wire bread ties, peels, eggshells, and so forth.

8

SPECIAL INTEREST IK TRIPS

Beyond the adventure and exhilaration IKs offer, they can also serve as an excellent vehicle for outdoor hobbies. For many paddlers, running the river is only a small part of the fun of their trip. Among other things, they use their IKs to access little-used fishing grounds, to travel to spectacular photographic areas, and to carry out interesting rocks.

IK FISHING

For certain applications, IKs make wonderful fishing boats. They are great for getting into remote areas where the fish haven't been spooked, or for accessing waters beyond the reach of ordinary boats. Remember that fishing from any kind of boat increases the amount of water you can cover in the time available and thereby increases your chances for success. Both beginners and experts can enjoy IK fishing trips. The trick is to tailor your trip to suit your fishing abilities and the type of fishing experience you desire.

Rivers suitable for IK travel vary widely in the types of fish they support. The most popular fish are trout and bass; some boaters also go for migratory fish like salmon and steelhead, or they go after fish that are not as glamorous, yet offer good eating, such as catfish.

Your technique and tackle will depend on the type of fish you're after, the kind of water you're on, and the kind of fishing experience you desire. The trick is in sneaking up on a fish and making a skilled cast to the spot where the fish is lurking. Some IK waters will be open for fly-fishing only, with other methods prohibited to preserve the fish population. Special break-down fly rods are available that will work well for IK trips. These are necessary, because a nine-foot rod would be too cumbersome on a small IK and apt to get broken. For spin or bait casting, you have a choice between a variety of break-down or telescoping rods. Usually the break-downs are better quality and more expensive, while the telescoping rods are much cheaper and easier to assemble. For casual IK fishing, a telescoping rod and modest reel are unbeatable. You can land some very nice fish on this light equipment.

Choose a rod with a carrying case, if possible, as this will help protect the rod from damage. A padded case is ideal. If your gear doesn't come with a protective case, you can improvise one by sewing up a nylon bag with ensolite foam inserts. Or use a section of PVC pipe for longer rods. Keep in mind that rods aren't the only fragile part of your fishing gear. Reels can be damaged if they are banged around. If the bail is bent, the reel may not work properly, so some kind of protection is necessary.

Besides rod and reel, you'll need line and tackle. Experienced anglers have their own preferences, which are likely to be suitable for IK fishing. Beginners may want to choose a heavy line (at least eight pounds) that helps prevent loss of fish and tackle while learning. A colored line, while possibly more visible to fish, helps a novice keep track of his or her line in the river.

For both fly and spin anglers, a small net may prove valuable for landing fish to the IK, especially if you want to keep your fish. Pulling a fish over the wide tubes of an IK may offer a chance for the fish to escape, because maintaining leverage against the fish is difficult while landing. Folding nets are practical choices, as are the very cheap small nets, which you don't worry about if you drop them overboard. Make sure any net is packed where the mesh won't entangle other gear, or the paddler in case of a flip. When purchasing tackle, don't forget a local fishing license.

Then you'll need something to carry your tackle in. Cheap sets that include rod, reel, and tackle are available but often are designed with children in mind. Although these look like nifty complete kits suitable for IK tripping, they are not likely to hold up for very long. More serious anglers may find a strap-on tackle box (produced by Berkley) very suitable for IK fishing. Not only is this container compact, it straps around your waist like a fanny pack. The box holds a surprising amount of gear and is "worm-proof." The opening is secure in whitewater and also allows the angler to fold down a work surface.

Small versions of regular tackle boxes also work on IK trips. Bear in mind that no tackle box is waterproof. In whitewater, tackle will get wet. Hooks, pliers, and other metal things may rust if not dried out properly. You may want to seal them in small waterproof containers like 35mm film cans. Another option is placing the entire tackle box inside a dry bag for the trip through whitewater. Rods and reels are usually not damaged by a dunking if you dry them out and oil the reel occasionally.

In calmer waters, your fishing equipment can ride unsecured in the floor of the IK or piled on the back. If rapids are to be encountered, though, plan on tying everything down beforehand. Make certain tackle boxes won't pop open under the pressure of pounding waves; you may want to fasten a strap around them for additional security. Hooks and lures are sharp and don't belong loose inside an air-filled boat.

On an IK trip, you usually have two options for fishing: from the IK as you float, or from shore (in camp or at a spot where you've landed). Generally, if you are running heavy rapids, or if you have a complicated angling system that requires time for assembly, then fishing from shore will be better for you. If you have a telescoping rod and are on an easy river where you don't need to worry much about raging rapids, then fishing while you drift is possible. Trolling—towing a flashy lure at a steady speed behind the boat—is sometimes tricky to manage in an IK, but an effective technique for getting fish. Paddling out to midstream or the opposite shore from your IK campground is also a worthwhile option because you can access more fishing waters, assuming you are camped near quiet waters. From a base camp, you can access rocky shorelines for bass, either from the boat or by walking.

An IK also serves as an excellent boat for solo anglers to use on ponds, sloughs, inlets, and other small waters, especially those where motors are impractical or not allowed. IKs are easy to launch, even without a paved ramp or other easy access. By using a rod holder and paddling at a steady clip, trolling is effective on flat water. Or sit in one spot and try jigging (moving the lure up and down); this is good for pond fish like crappie.

Naturally, there won't be much room in an IK for casting and landing fish. If you're new to fishing, learn to cast from shore before you take your modest skills onto the open water. Even veteran anglers will find it tougher to fish from an IK than from a motorboat. An IK will want to spin in circles or turn in the direction opposite your cast, when it's released from the discipline of the paddle. This is to be expected. Remember that an IK offers access to fishing waters, not a world-class platform to fish from. Some clever paddlers design a platform that fits across their IK with rudders for no-hands control, or with a rod-holder that allows them to keep the IK on track (not suitable for running whitewater). If you must steer the IK while angling, try holding your fishing rod between your legs, or tucking it under a strap. If an approaching obstacle is serious enough to merit both hands on the paddle, it's best to reel in your line. For whitewater, take down the rod well in advance of the rapid, and stow it securely.

On a river, the best places to fish are eddies along shore or behind rocks, where fish linger to rest and to feed. Try your luck at the tail-out of waves, too. Calm pools below rapids can be excellent fishing. About the only place you won't want to cast into is swift or rough waters, where your line will snag. Usually, fish there will be too busy fighting the current to respond to your offering. Smallmouth bass in rivers congregate around areas with large rocks in the water, even concrete pillars from old bridges. In an IK, you can paddle right into a midstream eddy or one of these rocky areas, but be careful not to spook the fish with a splash of the paddle or the shadow of your boat. Many fish that are easily spooked by an angler approaching from shore may be approached successfully from an IK in the water, if you go slowly.

Whether or not you keep the fish you catch depends on local regulations, the kind of fish, how badly the fish is hooked, and your personal philosophy. Native trout should always be released, unless they are too damaged to live. You can tell a native from a hatchery fish by checking the fins; hatchery fish often have fins clipped or worn away. Native fish are more colorful, too—look for the red slash on the gills that signals a cutthroat trout. Consult your local fish and wildlife office for further information on identifying native fish.

There are as many ways to cook a fish as there are to catch one. Unless you're avoiding calories, the tastiest way to cook your catch is deep-frying with tempura or other batter as a coating. Use fillets cut into bite-sized pieces for this. Coat each chunk of fish thoroughly with batter by dunking it, then immerse in hot vegetable oil. Drain (on paper towels or a tempura rack) and serve with lemon juice or tartar sauce as a dip. Small fish not filleted can be coated with a mix of cornmeal, flour, and seasonings, then pan-fried in margarine or vegetable oil. Fish may be baked on coals (in foil or "planked" on a flat surface), steamed, used in stir-fry dishes, barbecued on a grill, or cooked in a Dutch oven (use a coating such as Shake n' Bake for this). Eating fish raw, sushi style, isn't recommended as many of our American fish—trout in particular—can harbor parasites, which must be killed by cooking.

ROCKHOUNDING

Because IK rivers typically wind through picturesque rocky canyons, opportunities to find interesting rocks and to learn first-hand about the geology are superb. For example, a trip on the Colorado through the Grand Canyon takes you past some of the oldest rocks on Earth. Taking a class in rock and mineral identification, or the basics of geology, will greatly enhance your enjoyment of the river experience.

Just about everyone likes to pick up pretty rocks, or those with an intriguing shape. Serious rockhounds bring their special pick-hammers along (with the point carefully padded, so it won't damage the IK) to reach below the surface and find hidden treasures. Some rivers harbor valuable gemstones, such as opal, while others may offer attractive rocks that can be converted into bookends, paperweights, and the like. All waterways have well-worn pebbles suitable for "worry rocks" (smooth stones you keep in your pocket to caress the stress away), "pet rocks," or as souvenirs of your trip. In addition, rocks can be appreciated without collecting them or using them.

Collecting rocks for your personal enjoyment is legal on most public lands (but not in national parks). On private lands, you will need to acquire permission from the property owner before you collect. If you intend commercial use of rocks or anything else collected on public lands, a permit is usually necessary. Check with the agency in charge of the land around the river you'll be floating before you launch your IK. Remember that collecting or disturbing artifacts (any man-made object more than fifty years old) on public lands is illegal. Enjoy Indian ruins or old pioneer cabins, and take as many pictures as you want, but don't raid what may be a valuable archaeological site.

In particular, be careful around Indian rock carvings known as petroglyphs, and paintings, known as pictographs. These are very fragile and easily destroyed by careless boaters. To record them, use a camera; don't try rubbings unless you have official approval. Some of these images are so delicate that even the oils from your hands may hasten their destruction—so don't touch. And never, ever, scratch your own petroglyph or initials near such a site. If you witness vandalism or pot-hunters along a river, report them to the proper authorities (and get photos, if you have a camera). These vandals are destroying your heritage.

GOLD PANNING

Panning for gold offers an exciting addition to your paddle adventure trip. The lure of gold is powerful—remember that this rare mineral once drew hundreds of thousands of people away from their comfortable homes and into frozen wildernesses. Yes, you can still strike it rich, mostly because the cost of gold keeps soaring. There is less gold out there, so it's harder to find, but the gold is worth more. Of course, gold panning is hard work, but it's also fun.

On most rivers, you are allowed to pan for gold. Check first on rivers that flow through private lands; the property owner may or may not own the river bed where gold is found. Some public rivers, such as California's Klamath River, have active gold mining claims staked out, where panning is forbidden. Check with government authorities in charge of the region you're interested in exploring before you pack your pan.

All you need to get started is a gold pan, available at most camping supply stores. A plastic pan goes against the "sourdough" tradition, but remember that most metal pans rust badly, and it's difficult to see flecks of gold against a rusty backdrop. Plastic pans are inexpensive, lightweight, and work well. Your pan needs to be black, so gold dust will be visible. A pair of tweezers and a small vial, for picking up tiny flecks and saving them, are standard. (Finding nuggets is rare these days, but you never know!)

The basic action of panning is simple and easy to learn. You can receive instruction from tourist gold panning demonstrations, rock and mineral clubs, or community college classes. In essence, all you do is scoop up some sand in the pan, add a little river water, then swirl the pan so that the heavier gold flecks settle to the bottom of the pan. Tilt the pan to allow lighter-weight sand to escape (gold is heavier than sand or gravel). Keep flushing, swirling, and tilting until there is just a little sand left in the bottom. Any shiny flecks remaining are likely to be gold. Of course, iron pyrite (fool's gold) closely resembles the real thing, as does mica (although it's much lighter and more brittle than gold). That's why a class to help you identify minerals is helpful. Gold panning is fun and exciting and, with a little luck, you can make enough of a profit to buy that new paddle you want.

BIRD WATCHING

Birds and waterways just go together naturally. Along a typical stretch of river, you may see kingfisher, several kinds of ducks and geese, herons and cranes, osprey ("fish hawks"), songbirds, and even eagles (both golden and bald). Birding has become a popular pastime, and there's no place like a river for sighting exotic birds. You can easily carry a pair of binoculars and a bird book in a protective container, ready to haul out at a moment's notice. (Besides looking at birds, binoculars also come in handy for scouting rapids.)

Even without binoculars, if you keep alert, you can recognize many kinds of birds. Some are known by their songs or calls. For instance, the kingfisher makes a distinct rattling noise when disturbed. Keep watch for nests in the trees (osprey build huge stick nests), and along wilderness cliff walls, where you may even spot eagle nests. Birds come to the river for food and drink, and are fairly easy to observe from an IK. But do not approach waterfowl that are nesting along shore or those with young; ducks and geese will abandon their young if spooked. Enjoy ducklings and goslings from a distance.

Many birds feed on fish or other water-dwelling animals. If you are extremely lucky, you may be paddling down a wild river someday (most likely in Alaska) and be treated to the sight of a bald eagle swooping down to grab a salmon. Osprey are more common than the eagle, and make spectacular dives to the river, snatching up fish and winging back to the nest. While drifting quietly, you may observe a great blue heron wading silently in the shadows on stilt legs, stalking an unsuspecting frog.

On shore, especially during hikes, you may see hawks, owls, vultures, and other birds of prey. They are drawn to the river in search of food, like the creatures they prey upon. Some rivers are virtual music boxes in the spring, with hundreds of singing birds competing for mates. A special experience is the song of the canyon wren. The bird is so tiny, it's hard to believe the volume it can produce. Canyon wrens inhabit the spectacular gorges where rivers run free, and their song expresses that freedom.

Another special river bird is the water ouzel, sometimes called a dipper (or even a "teeterbutt"). The ouzel is a genuine whitewater bird, a bird that nests behind waterfalls or at the edge of raging rapids. Watching ouzels feed their young is nothing short of amazing. These little gray birds, which look somewhat like a sparrow, actually dive below the surface to gather insects for their hungry babies. They go right into whitewater after the bugs. This is a bird that an IK paddler can really identify with!

IK PHOTOGRAPHY

Most paddlers like to record their trips on film. A few even aspire to sell photographs of their adventures. However, many paddlers leave their cameras at home simply because they worry about getting them wet. The scenery, wildlife, and action of an IK adventure cries out for photographs. As for protecting the camera from spray, there are several good options.

First, consider a good, solid waterproof container for your camera. An ammo can offers superb water and shock protection for even the best of cameras. Although available used as Army surplus, the best—and most reliable—ammo cans come from river runner suppliers, at very reasonable prices. If you use such a box, pad it carefully inside and out, to protect both you and your camera from damage. Ensolite pads, cut to size and glued in place, are good for this. You

An ammo can is bulky, but perfect for protecting a camera from spray and banging around in the IK.

may want to paint it white or silver to increase visibility and reflect the sun's rays, which keeps the contents of the box cooler. Strap or tie the box down securely in the back of your IK where you can reach it. Two straps—one to secure the top, a second to fasten the side handle—make access easier. Such a box can also hold such valuables as wallets and car keys. Also available are the inflatable waterproof pouches for cameras. They are safer to have in the IK, but do not offer instant access like the ammo can. Choose one intelligently, as the cheap vinyl types can develop leaks or be easily torn.

Innovative camera technology has given photographers other options for taking pictures in wet conditions. Waterproof cameras range from the cheap and simple point-and-shoot types like Kodak's disposable housed in a plastic box (which even takes photos underwater), to moderately priced 35mm cameras like the Nikon Action Touch and the Minolta Weathermatic, to the pricey, top-quality divers' cameras like the Nikonos.

A waterproof housing for your everyday camera is another possibility to consider. And some folks swear by taking an old, inexpensive camera down the river—one that won't be missed if it goes overboard. It all depends on what you want to do with your photos. If you just want some snapshots of your trip and your companions, an inexpensive camera will suffice. If you dream of selling white-water photographs, get a good camera. A 35mm camera is the best choice for river trip photography, because with this format, you can get a good camera that fits into a small box, and you can use interchangeable lenses for different effects. They also have the fast shutter speeds necessary for good action shots; often the lenses on cheap cameras are too slow to freeze an IK crashing through a big wave. Most 35mm cameras aren't difficult to use, especially those with automatic exposure. Additionally, 35mm is the smallest format that most commercial photo buyers, like magazines, will accept for publication. You can teach yourself 35mm photography readily enough, or you might want to take some classes to better understand the basic photographic techniques: interchangeable lenses, f-stops, shutter speeds, depth of field, and so forth.

Incidentally, the best whitewater action shots are almost always taken from shore. In an IK, with the spray all around you, both hands need to be on the paddle. You don't want a camera strap hanging around your neck, as this might choke you. Some ingenious paddlers use duct tape to attach a waterproof camera to the middle of their paddle, so they can shoot pictures without missing a stroke. Others tuck a small camera inside their life jacket, where it can be whipped out for quick photos. (Even a waterproof camera should be wrapped in a Zip-Loc baggie for this, because water droplets on the lens will show up on your photos, and often, in an IK, there's nothing dry to use to wipe the lens clean. A piece of chamois cloth, however, may remove droplets even when wet—like a wet sponge.)

To get great action shots from shore, you need to be in position ahead of other paddlers. Unless you are the lead boat, you might want to walk around with the camera, take pictures of other boats coming through, then put the camera away when it's your turn to paddle (or let someone walk back upstream and photograph you in your boat). Trying to paddle ahead and set up for pictures can be difficult; not everyone wants to wait around while the photographer gets ready. Another alternative is to take the day off from paddling and set up your photography gear next to a well-traveled rapid. You might even sell some prints to the paddlers who come through.

Use a zoom or telephoto lens for good photos from shore, unless you can get very close to where the action is happening in the rapid. The zoom is more versatile, because you can pull back the lens to include all the faces on a big raft, or focus in tight on a small IK surfing a big wave. Long lenses make the whitewater look more exciting and magnify peoples' faces, creating better pictures. Also, a tripod to steady the long barrel of a zoom lens will produce sharper photos.

The best times to take pictures are early morning and late afternoon. During midday, you may have to deal with glare off the water. Good pictures are still possible, but remember that your camera's automatic light meter may be fooled by sunlight on whitewater. You may have to switch over to manual, or stop down the lens to outwit the "smart" camera. When shooting action shots, or taking pictures in your IK, always try to use a fast shutter speed, at least 1/125, preferably 1/250. These speeds freeze action, so every droplet of spray is crystal-clear. This is especially important when photographing from the IK—remember that an inflatable floating on water is creating motion around the camera, so you need to compensate for this.

When taking photos from a floating boat, try using a wide angle lens, at least 28mm. Leave the lens focused on infinity, and with an automatic camera, you're ready for instant, no-fuss scenics. Include a boat in pictures showing deep canyons—it adds to the perspective. The wide angle's generous and forgiving focus helps you get boat, cliff walls, and river all in sharp detail. A 35mm lens is almost as good, and is standard on many "point-and-shoot" cameras. Kodak also makes a Stretch disposable camera that takes super-wide photos, wonderful for capturing big canyon country.

If all you want are snapshots, use color print film. Easiest of all are the disposable cameras, which go back to the processor, film, camera, and all—no loading or unloading! However, if you want top-quality pictures, great colors, or are interested in selling your photos to publications, then you should learn to use color slide film. Kodachrome 64 is a wonderful film for shooting water photos, although good light is essential. Full sunlight is best when using this film. You'll find that warm colors—red, orange, and yellow life jackets and IKs—appear especially bright with Kodachrome. Scenic river canyons and colorful wildflowers look true to life as well. The drawback to Kodachrome 64 is its slow speed; on a cloudy day, it's useless.

Generally, beginners are better off with faster print films—even those with an ASA (film speed) of 100 cover a broad range of lighting. Faster films are more reliable than slower films in deep-canyon lighting conditions and are better able to capture fast whitewater action. Remember that slide films leave little latitude for exposure errors. When shooting slide film, always bracket your exposures (take one picture at the recommended exposure, then shoot one at a half or full stop above this, and one below).

Shooting green forests or blue waters? Then Ektachrome or Fujichrome is better, especially the faster versions that allow picture-taking under varied light conditions. For cloudy days or fast action, choose a film with a speed of ASA 200 to 400. Faster ASAs are available, up to 1,000 these days, but you pay a lot for these films, and the results are often grainy. Save them for those telephoto shots of bighorn rams way up on the cliff walls.

Faster-speed Kodachrome is available these days, with an ASA of 200 instead of 64. The results are almost as pleasing as 64 speed, and the film can be used in a broader range of lighting conditions.

You can minimize the risks of camera damage by being careful with your gear, whether it's waterproof or not. Keep unprotected cameras stowed while running rapids, and hold them over the boat when taking pictures on the water. Attach flotation straps to waterproof cameras so they won't sink. Label everything with your name and address in case something gets lost. Open up your camera containers at the end of the day to let any accumulated moisture evaporate. And, before your trip, take out a "floater" policy (no pun intended!) with your insurance company, so if you do drop a $300 camera into the river, you can buy another one right away.

WRITE ON THE RIVER

Another way to preserve memories of your adventures is to keep a journal. Writing on a river trip is demanding. It takes commitment. In camp, it's much easier to go for a swim or go off on a hike than it is to sit down and record the day's events. Nevertheless, if you force yourself to keep a journal, you'll enjoy the results later. Having a record of your adventures allows you to relive them later, especially if you go on many trips. And who knows? You might even compile a book about your adventures some day!

Special waterproof notebooks and writing instruments are available these days. You can also get a paddler's journal, in which you just fill in the blanks. Whatever you use, take a backup pencil in case your main pen runs dry or gets lost.

What to enter in a journal? On a new river, you might record mileages, names of major rapids and geographic features, wildlife sighted that day, remarks of other people on the trip, and your own impressions and feelings. Use all your senses when recording in a journal. Try to evoke the sharp smell of damp sagebrush in the desert air, the roar of the river at the big drop, the silky-soft feel of the sand on the beaches.

Some writers have begun to tote small word processors and mini computers down the river with them. Several of these "electronic notebooks" function entirely on battery power. These allow a novelist to continue work while on vacation. With the same protective ammo cans that keep cameras dry, carrying these high-tech toys is entirely feasible, especially if your IK trip is raft supported. Make sure the container is well-padded and that the computer fits into the container properly. And, just in case, have the computer insured. A buyer protection plan also comes in handy should you drop sensitive electronics into the sand.

9

RIVER INFORMATION GUIDE

A plethora of river guidebooks is available to aid you in your search for wilderness paddling adventures. When deciding on a river, you'll want to consider your skill level, the difficulty rating of the river, and the different factors of gradient, volume, degree of remoteness, terrain, float season, water temperature, and so forth. Try to choose a trip that suits both your needs and skills. You may be limited by geography or time, which will help narrow your choices.

Finding information on rivers not commonly floated is harder; you may have to spend a lot of time in the library looking up maps and tracking down specifics. For IK paddling, even a good guidebook may not eliminate all guesswork. A river might be described as "unfloatable" below a certain water level, when in fact that may be the case—for rafts. With an IK, the river may be quite "do-able." But, before you begin to explore rivers with little paddling information available, you will need to become experienced. When no guidebook offers a route through a rapid for you, you must be able to make that decision yourself.

ACCESS

Obviously, access is of prime importance; a river you can't get your boat onto isn't of much interest. Several factors restrict boater access: private lands, impassable terrain, and permit systems.

Most of the good wilderness waterways of the West flow through public lands, often under the jurisdiction of the U.S. Forest Service or the Bureau of Land Management (BLM). These waterways are national treasures that belong to everyone. Access, however, can be a different matter entirely. A river can be in public ownership, yet have no legal access for the public. When you research a river, check on access, keeping in mind that laws of public access vary from state to state. For instance, in Oregon, the state (the public) owns all the water in rivers and streams. It's perfectly legitimate for paddlers to float any river, even one that runs entirely through private lands, provided they don't trespass by launching on private property, or by landing on shore, according to river recreation instructor Mel Jackson. Even running aground or wading would be considered trespassing, because the land owner actually owns the riverbed. In some areas boaters are allowed only on what's considered a "navigable" river, a pretty limited definition, as no consideration is given to small boats as a legitimate use of a waterway. (Oregon considers a river navigable if it has a history of being used to float logs to timber markets.)

Another criteria commonly used to divide private property from public domain is the high-water line. In many areas, especially ocean beaches, the public has unrestricted access to waters up to the high-water line—but no further. You wouldn't be able to launch an IK into an ocean, river, or lake falling under this statute, unless the launch site was clearly labeled public land or you had permission to cross private property. However, landing or camping below the high-water line would be allowed.

Even if the area where you plan to launch is accessible to the public, getting your boat down to the water can be a problem, especially near the wilder rivers without boat ramps. When you get away from the developed areas, you'll really appreciate the IK's portability. If the access isn't too steep, an inflated IK can be carried down to the river without too much trouble. In really rugged country, carrying to the water's edge may be easier if the IK is deflated and rolled up into a bundle; you can always pump it up on the spot. This method is also helpful if the access is so brush-choked that a fully inflated IK might get snagged.

RIVER PERMITS

The third restriction on access—permit-only entry—can be harder to overcome than problems of land ownership or terrain. While rivers described extensively in guidebooks almost always have good access, many have become so popular with boaters that access has been limited to preserve the wilderness experience. Big-name rivers like the Colorado through the Grand Canyon in Arizona, Idaho's Salmon and Middle Fork, and Oregon's Rogue now limit the numbers of boaters who are allowed on the river at any one time. Boaters who desire to float these rivers must enter a lottery months in advance (or even years, for the Colorado) of their planned trip. The only exceptions are boaters who plan on floating with one of the commercial outfitters permitted on the river of their choice. Authorized outfitters are limited to launching on certain dates and also have party-size restrictions to abide by.

The river permit system is far from perfect. Many private boaters loathe the idea of restricted access, especially since commercial outfitters often get the lion's share of the available spaces, even if there are no float trip customers to fill them. But, until needed changes in the system occur, if you plan a trip on a limited-access river you will need to get a permit.

The traditional process involves sending your application in, and having all your friends submit applications, too. Several of the government agencies in charge of permit-controlled rivers have begun to charge a fee for applications, to discourage multiple applications by less-than-serious boaters. But there are other ways to get on the river. If your schedule is flexible, it's often possible to wait at the river on stand-by basis, taking the place of anyone who doesn't show up. Or you can contact successful permit-holders and try to join their trip.

Still another avenue exists for skilled IK paddlers. On some rivers, the float season for traditional craft is relatively short. For example, on the Selway River, Idaho's coveted wilderness run, the permit-only season ends July 31 because the river is too low for both rafting and enjoyable hardshell kayaking after that time, but a group of experienced IK paddlers could make a go of it, without the bother of permits. Other rivers are just not as desirable at certain times of the year, usually late in the season when the water is getting low. Few boaters will want permits then, particularly during a drought year, but the decreased water levels may be made-to-order for IKs.

Keep in mind, also, that the IK's ability to run at low-water levels opens up many rivers and streams that don't require permits simply because the crowds can't get down them. Desert rivers that drop off in late spring or early summer, for example, offer wonderful paddling for IKs beyond the normal season. However, you have to use good judgment to distinguish a river that is presumed unrunnable below a certain level from a river that really is unrunnable. As a general rule, IKs can run at water levels one-half to two-thirds lower than the suggested minimum flow for other boats.

Among many boaters, a bias against gentle streams exists. Some macho paddlers wouldn't be caught dead on anything less than a raging Class IV river. This is their loss and a big gain for IK paddlers, who know how to find joy and challenge in running any wild, scenic river. Remember that the very nature of IKs, in which you are seated close to the water with your face in the spray, amplifies the size and fury of rapids. What might bore a boater in a fifteen-foot raft can be a real blast in an IK. Don't overlook the easier waters, even when you're an experienced boater.

RESEARCHING A RIVER

Before you float, you should find out what to expect. What class are the rapids? Will you be able to portage or line around the tough rapids? Are there waterfalls, or maybe even sheer-walled, impassable gorges? How rocky is this river at the water level you intend to float, and can your IK handle the abuse? Where could you walk out for help, if an emergency occurs?

Much of this information is covered in guidebooks. On more exotic rivers, you'll have to find out for yourself. In Alaska, where bush planes are necessary to access many wilderness rivers, paddlers commonly fly over the river they wish to float for a quick preview. This way, they can spot any log jams or other hazards from the air, and safely avoid them, or change rivers if the one they have in mind seems too difficult. Unless you can afford a private plane or helicopter, though, you may have to rely on library research. One alternative is hiking to the river before your trip; this is good for previewing rapids in deep gorges. Take a pair of binoculars for this.

Talking with people who've run the river is always a good idea, but be wary of believing everything you hear. Some folks delight in sending beginning paddlers into hairy whitewater. Others, especially commercial outfitters, tend to overrate the dangers involved (obviously, they want you to go on their paid trip, rather than make the run on your own). It's best to talk to several people, then average the reports.

When planning a trip, keep in mind that the primary limitation on any float adventure is the speed of the current. On an average whitewater river that drops around twenty feet per mile, you can figure on covering ten to twenty miles per day, depending on how early you get started, how often and how long you stop, the wind, and so forth. Usually, a daily limit of about fifteen miles is suitable. On slower rivers, plan for fewer miles each day. Allow enough time

for scouting rapids and for lounging in camp and indulging in hobbies. Layover days, where no mileage is made, are worthwhile on
longer trips. Choose a site where there is ample hiking, a hot spring,
or other interesting diversions to explore.

TRANSPORTATION

Getting to the river can be more of a problem than you imagine,
depending on where the river is located. You can drive your own car
or share with others. If ground transportation is available, you might
take a commercial airliner. Public transportation may take you right
to the launch site, especially in a national park. In some remote
regions, you must fly in via bush plane. And, with a lightweight IK
and gear, it's entirely possible to pack into the head of a river using
horses, mules, llamas, or mountain bikes to help carry the load.

Arranging for a shuttle—transportation back to your vehicle—is
usually necessary. Running the shuttle is routine along rivers regularly floated; you'll find entire industries sprung up around shuttle
services. Shuttle costs vary widely, depending on the number of
miles the shuttle driver must travel, how rough the road is, and
whether or not a second vehicle is required to bring the driver back.
You can run your own shuttle if you have two cars, but this takes
time away from your trip. Although the easiest shuttle is an extended
thumb, there aren't many cars to pick up hitchhikers in the backcountry, especially if you get off the river late in the day. If you ever
find yourself hitchhiking a shuttle, wear your PFD so you'll look like
a nonthreatening paddler, rather than a crazed axe murderer. In
areas around popular rivers, boaters should pick up other boaters.

On a river where few or no boaters run, there may not be an established shuttle service. Look for a responsible local person, such as
a waitress, who might be interested in driving your car back for a
reasonable fee. Most small town workers are willing to help you out.

For a short shuttle, you may be able to spot a bicycle at the end
of the trip. If the trip requires driving past the take-out spot first and
then going on to the launch site, using two cars is more feasible.
Another option is having a person along who doesn't go on the
float trip; he or she just drives the car back, and maybe meets the
boaters for lunch, if there is road access. On rivers with sufficient
road access, this makes camping a cinch. Gear rides in the shuttle
vehicle and arrives in camp each night, while the IKs ride high and
light over the waves.

CONSERVATION

Every paddler must be involved in keeping wild rivers wild. Beyond picking up litter and using firepans, paddlers need to lobby to have more rivers placed under the protection of the National Wild and Scenic Rivers Act. Otherwise, your favorite river might be next on the chopping block.

To keep abreast of the latest developments in river conservation, you'll want to join an organization like Friends of the River or the National Organization for River Sports (NORS). This is a good way to meet other paddlers, organize trips, and help to preserve our dwindling supply of wild rivers.

But, rather than just sending in your dues, if you like paddling and exploring wild rivers, try to work on river protection legislation. Write your congressional representatives about every proposed dam that threatens a local river. Write letters to the editor of the newspaper when rivers are threatened with destruction. Send in your comments when a river is being studied for possible inclusion in the Act, and attend meetings where the fate of wild rivers is being decided. Be a watchdog over corporations and industries that might pollute your favorite river, and let them know you're watching them.

Once a river is destroyed, it can never be restored.

10

PADDLING ON OCEANS AND LAKES

Because IKs are so well suited to river exploration, their other uses are often overlooked. But the IK is a versatile craft, equally at home on the broad expanse of a lake or in ocean surf. Inflatables offer some specific advantages over hardshell boats. For example, they are a good choice for landing in rocky areas with rough surf—conditions such as those found along the wilderness shorelines of Hawaii—because the air-filled boat bounces off rocks, unlike the traditional wood outrigger canoe. Also, should the whole boat dump upsidedown in strong surf, the inflatable hull is far less likely to injure a paddler. And a self-bailing IK won't swamp in heavy surf. IKs are perfect for pack trips into remote lakes, and for transporting by airplane, because they roll into small bundles.

Have an idea of what your IK can handle before you plan a lake or, especially, an ocean expedition. Nearly all IKs can handle ponds, sloughs, easy rivers, and mild whitewater, but not every IK is built to withstand the pounding of rough seas. In some conditions, you may need braces to help you stay in the boat. If the water is very cold, you may need to deck over your open cockpit and wear a wetsuit or drysuit.

Remember that on a large lake far from shore, you are isolated. Stormy weather can quickly turn a placid lake into choppy waves capable of swamping or overturning an IK. What looked like an easy paddle across the lake can suddenly turn into an exhausting marathon should the wind pick up, or reverse direction. Fatigue can leave you stranded, as can a leaky boat.

Of course, the techniques for paddling an IK will differ when switching from moving current to slack water, or when dealing with the special problems surf presents. Before you head out for open waters, practice paddling on ponds or inlets to get a feel for how the IK will handle without a current. Before you get serious about sea kayaking, do some research; practice in quiet areas, and try to join an experienced sea kayaking group for your initial expeditions. As with rivers, gain knowledge slowly. If you are sincerely interested in sea kayaking, seeking professional instruction hastens the learning process while increasing safety. You may be expected to use a hard-shell kayak instead of your own IK, but the techniques are similar and will transfer. The most important part of sea kayaking fits not in your boat, but in your head: knowledge of tides and their effects on ocean currents, a rudimentary understanding of seaside meteorology, and a grounding in the basics of navigation with compass and charts.

Instead of rocks and rapids, waves and wind will be your biggest problems when paddling lakes and oceans. Both will affect your IK differently than they did while on the river. However, you can use your river skills to cope with these problems. Or, if you begin on lakes or oceans, the paddling skills you pick up there will come in handy should you decide to explore a river.

DEALING WITH WIND

You can help counter the wind problem by choosing longer IKs, especially models designed for sea kayaking. These will track better on flatwater. In a headwind (blowing towards you), shift weight forward so that the bow of the IK rides lower in the water and doesn't catch as much wind. You might want to stack full one-gallon water jugs into the bow, or try shifting your body weight farther forward. When the wind reverses and blows from behind you, do just the opposite: lighten the bow, so it will act like a sail, pushing the IK forward.

Also, you should feather your paddle in a headwind, but use it unfeathered in a tailwind (the extra paddle surface exposed to the wind helps to propel you). Try to plan ocean or lake trips around the wind, if possible. Around islands like Hawaii, the wind often blows predictably in one direction; if you launch and land following this steady breeze, the trip will be much easier.

If the wind suddenly becomes strong, it's best to head for shore and not risk paddling against it. Will a sail help? Probably not, unless you can rig a rudder. IKs are difficult to sail, as they lack the devices that keep them going in the right direction, such as a rudder, keel, or skeg. These act much like the paddle blade during a rudder stroke, and are standard equipment on many hardshell flatwater boats. It's possible to rig such a device to some IKs to improve sailing and drifting in the right direction, allowing you to relax your paddling as you would in a gentle river current. (A keel can be added to AIRE's Lynx.) In a pinch, try positioning your paddle blade as a rudder well behind you, near the end of the stern.

Of course, with a really strong wind behind you, any flat surface held high, even a shirt, will catch wind and push you forward.

STAY IN SIGHT

Keep close to shore (but out of heavy surf) when paddling on oceans or lakes. It's easy to become disoriented and lose your way. If you must cross a lake, sight in on a landmark and paddle straight across to it, or take bearings on a compass. Unless you are a very skilled adventurer, when you're on the ocean, never paddle an IK out of sight of land. Ocean paddling is best confined to quiet inlets, bays, and river mouths, until you have gained the experience to deal with surf and undertows. Even paddling around the shoreline of an island takes skill; you must launch and land through the surf line, and this is where most upsets happen.

The danger of paddling across a big lake is that you have no cover should a storm begin brewing. Try to make a crossing only in good weather. If stuck in a storm, paddling may become impossible in the heavy waves. You may have to wait it out. It's possible to rig an anchor, using a water jug or similar weight, that keeps an IK from being tossed around too much. A sea anchor (such as a bucket on a rope) helps to slow you down if your boat is being dragged out to open sea. Also, it's possible to overestimate how far you can paddle on open waters. Because there is no helpful current pushing you along, paddling can be more taxing. Should a strong wind come up unexpectedly, this will slow you down even further. Keep the limitations of flatwater in mind when planning a lake trip.

Another problem in open waters can arise if you get tossed out of the IK. Wind or waves can carry an IK far from your hands faster than you would believe. Paddles present the same problem; they're easily lost to an ocean current. The solution is to use *clip lines*. While attaching a line between yourself and your gear is strictly forbidden on rivers, this practice makes sense on open water. Fasten one line from your paddle to your boat (some paddlers attach their paddles to one wrist) and another line from your PFD to your boat. If you lose your boat or paddle on open water, it's a long swim to shore. These lines are sometimes called clip lines because most paddlers prefer to use a spring clip instead of knots to fasten the line to themselves; this way, freeing yourself to go ashore is less trouble. Don't use a long, cumbersome line that will wrap around everything—keep it short. Light shock cord or similiar line works well. Some sea kayakers use a household broom clip on a line as a "paddle park" so they can set their paddles safely aside while taking pictures, rescuing another boater, or enjoying a rest. Never let go of an unsecured paddle, because a stray wave or blast of wind could steal it away from you.

Some paddlers argue that you shouldn't be connected to a heavy boat while attempting a rough landing, because if you dump out, the boat can smash against you, or squash you between it and a jagged rock. However, an IK is lighter and much less likely to injure you in such a situation, unless very heavily loaded, or swamped with water. You can lessen this risk, though, by unclipping yourself beforehand. First, weigh the risk of the boat (and load) harming you against the risk of losing all your gear to the surf. In isolated regions, such as an island or beneath unscalable cliffs, you could become stranded without survival equipment, or the means to escape. Under such conditions, you're much better off staying with your boat and gear.

On the ocean, always carry some sort of emergency signaling device—for example, flares, foghorn, or radio transmitter—so if you get into trouble, you can broadcast your distress. Signals for a trip across a big lake also aren't a bad idea, but if the lake is pure wilderness, there may not be anyone around to view your flares. Also, if the water is cold, carry matches and firestarter, a space blanket or other shelter, the makings for hot drinks, and spare warm clothing.

SURF'S UP

Riding ocean waves in an IK offers plenty of thrills and maybe some spills. Before you tackle surf, you need to understand ocean conditions, especially how tides work. A tidal table and waterproof watch will prove useful. You may need to use a crash helmet for surfing or landing along rocky coastlines. Go with other boaters and have a spotter on shore to keep an eye on everyone in the surfing group. Practice in small surf, then work your way up to the bigger stuff gradually. Stay in bays or other calm areas until you build skill and confidence in riding the waves and paddling your IK through the surf. Never attempt to paddle the ocean during bad weather; a storm can create huge surf in just a few hours' time. Before you tackle ocean paddling, make sure you're in shape. You will need strength, endurance, and experience to paddle through crashing surf.

Waves vary in shape and size. You need to learn to read the ocean, just as you would a river. Look for waves that beckon surfers with smooth, regular surfaces. Avoid waves that develop breaking crests, much like a river's backcurling waves; these can trash an IK. Wave configurations are influenced by such factors as the shape of beaches, winds, and tides. With practice, you can learn to predict when and where good surf conditions will appear. For example, a flat beach offers gentler waves than a steep beach does.

Ocean conditions can change very quickly, from calm surf to raging swells in just a few hours, so you need to be alert and get accurate weather forecasts before your trip. Surf conditions also vary with the season and the time of day; expect higher, rougher surf in winter.

Beginners should look for a sheltered bay with small waves, from two to four feet high. Spilling breakers in the six to eight foot range are powerful and can easily overturn an IK. The size of waves far from shore may be difficult to determine until the waves are very close. Beware of huge rogue waves!

Unlike board surfers, IK boaters should always wear their PFDs. Many board surfers disdain life jackets because they feel such protective devices aren't macho, and also because they fear the additional flotation will bring them to the surface too quickly, which might bring their heads into contact with their surfboards. IKs, however, being soft craft, don't present this problem. The PFD offers extra security in big waves and protection from hypothermia, a potential problem in all but the warmest waters.

On the open ocean, beyond the shore's surf line, you will find a choppy sort of water that rocks you in your IK like a baby in a cradle. This movement of the ocean underneath you is ground swell. Most swells are gradual and no problem for IKs. Yet, because the motion is side-to-side, seasickness can be a problem for some. If bothered, try over-the-counter pills or consult a physician for a more modern preventative, such as a patch positioned near your ear that reportedly eliminates seasickness in most individuals.

Surf is created as swells approach a shoreline. Waves grow in size, crashing and reforming, then gradually diminish as they near the shore. Surprisingly deceptive force lurks behind even a small surf. Before you can explore what lies beyond the surf line, you must first learn how to deal with this force.

ESCAPING SURF

On any ocean voyage, paddlers who want to travel, rather than just play in the waves, must deal with escaping the continuous pounding action of the surf. To paddle around an island, for example, you must first launch an IK off the beach, then paddle through and past incoming waves. Then you must be able to return to shore safely, which means another trip through the surf line. Getting through surf can be difficult and demanding, depending on how rough the waves are and how good a paddler you are.

As you would on the river, scout your run beforehand. Look for a break in the surf that will make paddling easier. Smaller waves offer safer, easier paddling than a direct route through strong surf. When you start, keep going—don't stop paddling, or you may ride the waves back to shore. Paddle quickly through the breakers until you reach calmer swells. As on a river, keep your IK headed straight into the waves, not sideways. Lean forward into the waves and keep your head down. If you get knocked sideways, lean away from the beach and brace to keep the IK upright, especially when coming back through surf.

When launching your boat, watch for a lull in the surf and be ready to move quickly when the waves die down. Waves run in sets, so time your launch to coincide with the last wave of a series. In tricky surf, you'll want to be sitting in your IK ready to paddle as the right moment approaches. For this to work, assistance from shore is usually necessary; find someone to hold your boat until you're ready to paddle. An experienced surf paddler can help beginners launch, but then must be able to solo launch after all the others are gone, unless a nonpaddler is available. Remember you must paddle fast and hard to clear breaking surf.

Landing in surf can be equally challenging. Judging the size of the waves from their backsides is often difficult. Wait for a lull in the action, if you can, before starting your entry. Be ready to paddle like mad when you spy an opening. Look for a good landing spot, such as a bay, where the surf is not as rough. You may have to stay on the back of a wave, especially in heavy surf; use your backpaddle stroke for this. Keep your distance from other boats to avoid collisions in surf. Be alert, too, for logs rolling around in surf. These kill unwary beachcombers along the unpredictable Pacific coast every year, and paddlers aren't exempt from this hazard.

Because IKs can easily swamp in big ocean waves, a self-bailer may perform better. An IK with a bow spray shield will resist "endoing" in the surf by keeping the nose of the boat from being plowed under. And an IK with a rigid ethafoam floor works better than one with an inflatable floor, especially for surfing waves—it's more like a real surfboard. You need a boat with high impact resistance and good stability when dealing with remote coastlines and big waves, particularly if you are forced to ram rugged lava rock while landing in heavy surf. There won't always be a friendly beach when you need to land the IK.

WHERE TO GO

Sea kayakers paddle everywhere from the San Francisco Bay and along the rugged Pacific coastline (wear a heavy wetsuit!) to balmy Hawaii and other tropical shores. Paddling along inlets or islands around Alaska is popular, as well. Lake paddlers have thousands of alternatives, from small wilderness waters to the Great Lakes. Conditions vary wildly, from bathwater temperatures in Hawaii to floating icebergs in parts of Alaska.

Where you go depends on what kind of experience you want to have. In Alaska, you can find wilderness beaches where you can live off the land, catching crabs and bottom fish in quiet bays. Remote areas in Hawaii offer much the same, only with tropical fruit for the plucking. The Boundary Waters Canoe Area offers miles of paddling, with some portaging between lakes.

BASIC SAFETY TIPS FOR OPEN WATERS

Besides your signaling devices, take plenty of water (never drink salty ocean water or sip from an open lake). Prepare for exposure; take sun lotion, hand lotion, Chapstick, and proper clothing. Watch out for motorboats; they may or may not see a small IK bobbing in the waves. A fast boat passing your IK can leave a hefty wake behind; prepare to meet the incoming waves head-on, just like on the river. Avoid paddling on big lakes with heavy motorboat traffic if you can. Some lakes are off-limits to motors, or to motors over a certain horsepower. Also avoid the shipping lanes, where a giant freighter could mow down both you and your IK.

Stay with your group. Always have yourself clipped to the boat when crossing open waters. Some paddlers remove their clip line when landing in heavy surf, with the idea that they don't want a heavy boat colliding with them. This is fine except in wilderness surf landings, when you can't risk losing your boat. As on a river trip, inform a responsible person when the group is leaving, when you expect to return, and what route you plan to take.

SPECIAL HAZARDS

Beyond the problems of surf and wind, paddlers on open water face some hazards most river paddlers would never dream of. For example, simple mud or tidal flats can be treacherous, sucking an unwary paddler down to his or her waist in muck, in seconds. Vast areas of what looks like innocent beach could be quicksand. Before you jump out of the IK, make sure the surface really is as solid as it appears. If caught, hold onto your boat and pull yourself out. Away from the boat, swim as though in water, with your weight spread out flat so you won't get sucked down.

Fog can quickly disorient a paddler. Rather than heading for shore, you could wind up paddling to Japan. Paddling through a heavy mist is a special experience, but use caution. Even fog on a lake can cause you to lose your way. A map and compass will help.

Icebergs may be encountered in the far north. Paddling close is very tempting, yet dangerous, as icebergs aren't the static lumps they appear to be. Smaller chunks of ice can unexpectedly fall off, in a process known as calving. You don't want to be in the way while an iceberg is giving birth to a two-hundred-pound offspring. And, although everyone knows icebergs hide most of their bulk under the surface, paddlers often don't realize that an iceberg can abruptly flip over. Generally, icebergs with jagged edges are more dangerous than smooth lumps of floating ice, as the smooth edges were softened by a previous dunking. Rough edges mean the iceberg may be due for a rollover.

Some animals in ocean waters are dangerous to unsuspecting paddlers. Avoid jellyfish; some, such as the Portuguese man-of-war, deliver nasty stings. They look like globs of jello with tentacles hanging below. The tenacles are venomous to varying degrees. Some individuals can have severe allergic reactions to such a sting.

The risk of sharks in open ocean waters has been exaggerated by scary movies, yet the threat to paddlers is real. Obviously, an IK offers little resistance to a determined shark. If you are planning to paddle in areas where sharks may be a problem, you may want to carry some self-defense. Shark repellent is available through Navy surplus or survival outlets, but its usefulness has never been proven. Hitting a shark sharply on its head is supposed to discourage them, so one veteran sea kayaker recommends a "bang stick" for paddlers to fend off sharks (the device uses a shotgun shell to dissuade the shark). Sharks are attracted by blood; if you are fishing, be extra careful with dead fish and fish guts thrown overboard or trolled next to your IK.

Like whitewater, open water has its risks—and its special rewards. Proceed at your own pace, but don't let fear enslave you!

"A man sits as many risks as he runs."

—Henry David Thoreau
Walden

APPENDIX

DAY TRIP CHECKLIST

___ IK
___ Paddle
___ PFD
___ Pump
___ Duct tape/repair kit
___ Small first aid kit
___ Lunch
___ Water bottle, full
___ Sunscreen
___ Spare clothing in case you get dunked or chilled, sealed in dry bag
___ Throwbag/rescue gear
___ Helmet (for rocky rivers)
___ Plastic scoop to use as bailer
___ River clothing suitable for conditions encountered
___ Footgear
___ Camera (optional) and case, if not waterproof
___ Matches, firestarter
___ Toilet paper
___ Wallet and keys

OVERNIGHT TRIP CHECKLIST

___ IK
___ Paddle and spare
___ PFD
___ Pump
___ Full repair kit
___ Full first aid kit
___ Lunches
___ Water bottle, full
___ Throwbag
___ Helmet (for rocky rivers)
___ Plastic scoop to use as bailer
___ Sunscreen

__ River clothing suitable for conditions encountered

__ Footgear

__ Extra clothing for camp

__ Camp shoes/thongs

__ Wallet and keys

__ Carabiner or pulley for rescues

__ Large dry bag for overnight gear

__ Ammo cans and/or small dry bags for miscellaneous items

__ Tent or bivy shelter

__ Sleeping bag

__ Air mattress or pad

__ Ground sheet or tarp to be used under/inside tent, extra for shelter

__ Chair (optional)

__ Table (optional)

__ Food

__ Cooking pots

__ Camp stove

__ Fuel

__ Flashlight/candle

__ Small candle or other lantern (optional)

__ First aid kit/emergency supplies (including space blankets)

__ One-gallon water jug, full

__ Basic kitchen gear: can opener, pot holder, knife, matches, eating utensils, seasonings, soap, and chlorine bleach, wash bucket or dishpans, water purification system

__ Fire pan or fire blanket

__ Map, guidebook, compass, tidal tables, etc.

__ Toilet paper/premoistened towelettes

__ Plastic trowel or folding shovel, or Porta-Potty System

__ Insect repellent

__ Garbage bags/Zip-Loc baggies

__ Signaling device, especially for remote areas: mirror (to flash aircraft), firearm, whistle, flares/flare gun, radio transmitter, smoke/dye device. Groups might investigate Morse code/Semaphore (flags) for signaling when separated by a river.

__ Basic toiletries: biodegradable soap, toothbrush and toothpaste, shaver, hand lotion, Chapstick, sun lotion, towel, feminine hygiene supplies

__ Optional: camera, film, gold pan, rock pick, fishing gear, books, magnifying glass, binoculars, notebook, solar shower, etc.

__ Cold weather: thermos with hot water, drink mixes

RIVER CONSERVATION ORGANIZATIONS

American Rivers
801 Pennsylvania Avenue SE
Suite 303
Washington, D.C. 20003
(202) 547-6900

American Whitewater Affiliation
136 13th Street SE
Washington, D.C. 20003
(202) 546-3766

Friends of the River
909 12th Street, Suite 207
Sacramento, California 95814
(916) 442-3155

The Nature Conservancy
1815 North Lynn Street
Arlington, Virginia 22209
(703) 841-5300

National Organization for
River Sports
P.O. Box 6847
314 North 20th Street
Colorado Springs, Colorado 80904
(719) 473-2466

Sierra Club
730 Polk Street
San Francisco, California 94109
(415) 776-2211

SOURCES OF IKS AND RIVER EQUIPMENT

Achilles Inflatable Craft
P.O. Box 2287
1407 80th SW
Everett, Washington 98203
(206) 353-7000
or
P.O. Box 517
East Rutherford, New Jersey 07073
(201) 438-6400 or 1-800-722-5232

*Produces tough 80 percent Hypalon IKs
in one- and two-person sizes.*

AIRE (Argonaut Inflatable Research
and Engineering)
P.O. Box 3412
Boise, Idaho 83703
(208) 344-7506

*Source for rugged, high-tech PVC/
urethane IKs with ethafoam floors and
unique "air bladder" system. Also available are the Sea Tiger self-bailing IK for
sea kayaking and custom thigh brace
kits.*

B & A Distributing Co.
201 Southeast Oak Street
Portland, Oregon 97214
(503) 230-0482

*Importer of medium-priced Riken and
Momentum Hypalon-coated IKs. Does
not sell retail, but can put you in touch
with dealer closest to your area. Offers
both self-bailing IKs and non-SBs for
paddlers who want to do their own SB
conversion and save some money. Source
for super-heavy-duty air mattress floors
suitable for sleeping pads, and sturdy
inflatable seats for IKs.*

The Boat People
Inflatable Kayak Specialists
3230 Segovia Court
San Jose, California 95127
(408) 258-7971

*The only supplier specializing in IKs.
Source for most major brands of IKs and
inflatable canoes. Also carries paddle-
boards, pumps, dry bags, paddles, soft
coolers, and anything else an IK paddler
could need. Catalog includes info-packed
IK specs chart. Does SB conversions.*

Boulder Outdoor Center, Inc.
2510 North 47th Street
Boulder, Colorado 80301
(303) 444-8420

*Source for kayak clothing and acces-
sories, and IK sales and rentals.*

Carlisle Paddles
4562 North Down River Road
P.O. Box 488
Grayling, Michigan 49738
(517) 348-9886

Source for break-down inflatable kayak paddles.

Cascade Outfitters
145 Pioneer Parkway East
P.O. Box 209
Springfield, Oregon 97477
(503) 747-2272 or 1-800-223-RAFT
(7238)

Catalog available. Source for PFDs, paddles, and other whitewater gear; also carries several top brands of inflatable kayaks and boater clothing.

Colorado Kayak Supply
P.O. Box 3059
Buena Vista, Colorado 81211

Source of IK accessories and river clothing as well as IK sales. Mail- order catalog available.

Demaree Inflatable Boats
P.O. Box 307
Friendsville, Maryland 21531
(301) 746-5815 or 1-800-342-8823

Manufacturer of rugged neoprene IKs called Dipper, Double Dipper, R-1 and R-2. Self-bailing models with inflatable floors.

Hyside Whitewater Inflatables (Formerly Sun Runner)
P.O. Box Z
Kernville, California 93238
(619) 376-3723

Source of Hypalon "Padillac" IKs.

Man of Rubber
Route 1, Box 93B
Reliance, Tennessee 37369
(615) 338-2775

Source for river equipment accessories and Zip-Dry bags.

Northwest Design Works, Inc.
12414 Highway 99 South #47
Everett, Washington 98204

Source for Werner custom paddles.

Northwest River Supplies
P.O. Box 9186
Moscow, Idaho 83843
(208) 882-2383 or 1-800-635-5202

Catalog available. Source of EPDM IKs, dry bags, paddles, PFDs, paddling clothes, etc.

Orange Torpedoes
P.O. Box 1111
Grants Pass, Oregon 97526
(503) 479-5061

Sole distributor of Sevylor's "semi-self-bailing" professional model Tahiti; these cost about $125, including two seats. Also conducts outfitted IK trips in Tahitis on northwest rivers.

Seattle Sports
2122 West Elmore
Seattle, Washington 98199
1-800-STA-KOLD
(206) 282-9965

Source of soft coolers, dry bags, and straps.

Sevylor U.S.A.
6651 East 26th Street
Los Angeles, California 90040
(213) 727-6013 or 1-800-821-4645

Manufacturer of Tahiti brand vinyl IKs, Sevytex reinforced vinyl IKs, air mattresses, paddles, etc.

Voyageur's
P.O. Box 409
Gardner, Kansas 66030
(913) 764-7755

Dry bags, camera bags, PFDs, helmets. Emphasis on hardshell boats.

Wildwater Designs
230 Penllyn Pike
Penllyn, Pennsylvania 19422
(215) 646-5034

Catalog available. Source for paddling gear.

SOURCES FOR CAMPING EQUIPMENT

Berkley
Outdoor Technologies Group
One Berkley Drive
Spirit Lake, Iowa 51360

Source for strap-on tackle box for IK fishing.

Campmor
810 Route 17 North
P.O. Box 997-C
Paramus, New Jersey 07653

Catalog available. Source for Katadyn water filter, heavy-duty rubberized canvas air mattresses, Lady J for women.

REI (Recreational Equipment Inc.)
P.O. Box 88125
Seattle, Washington 98138
1-800-828-5533

Catalog available. Source for lightweight backpacker gear, useful gadgets, some river gear.

IK INSTRUCTION AND OUTFITTERS

Adventure Kayaking International
P.O. Box 61609
Honolulu, Hawaii 96822
(808) 988-3913
1-800-63-ISLES

Day, overnight, and multiday trips around Hawaiian Islands; also offers rentals and information.

Beyond Limits
P.O. Box 215
Riverbank, California 95367
(209) 529-7655

IK trips on Class II and Class III rivers in California.

Eastern Professional River
Outfitters Association
531 South Gay Street, Suite 600
Knoxville, Tennessee 37902
(615) 524-1045

Source for information about dozens of outfitters in the East.

Rusty Banana Ocean Adventures/Go Bananas
740 Kapahulu
Honolulu, Hawaii 96815

Offers tours, sales, and rentals of IKs in Hawaii.

Western River Guides
Association, Inc.
360 South Monroe, Suite 300
Denver, Colorado 80209
(303) 377-4811

Source for information about dozens of outfitters across the West.

Wild Water Adventures
P.O. Box 249
Creswell, Oregon 97426
(503) 895-4465 or 1-800-289-4534

Inflatable kayak instruction and schools, all-IK trips on wilderness rivers, raft-supported IK trips on the Rogue, Klamath, and other rivers. Uses self-bailing Hypalon IKs.

READING MATERIAL

Kayak Technique

Nealy, William. *Kayak: The Animated Manual of Intermediate and Advanced Whitewater Technique*. Menasha Ridge Press.

Tejada-Flores, Lito. *Wildwater: The Sierra Club Guide to Kayaking and Whitewater Boating*. Sierra Club Books.

Kayak Touring

Daniel, Linda. *Kayak Cookery: A Handbook of Provisions and Recipes*. Pacific Search Press.

Hutchinson, Derek C. *Derek C. Hutchinson's Guide to Sea Kayaking*. Globe Pequot Press.

Sutherland, Audrey. *Paddling Hawaii*. The Mountaineers.

Sanders, William. *Kayak Touring*. Stackpole Books.

General Whitewater Boating

Bechdel, Les, and Slim Ray. *River Rescue*. Appalachian Mountain Club.

Jacobson, Cliff. *Canoeing Wild Rivers*. ICS Books.

Kuhne, Cecil. *Advanced River Rafting*. Anderson World, Inc.

McGinnis, William. *Whitewater Rafting*. Times Books.

Watters, Ron. *The White-Water River Book*. Pacific Search Press.

Paddle Adventures

DuBois, Eliot. *An Innocent on the Middle Fork: A Whitewater Adventure in Idaho's Wilderness*. The Mountaineers.

Goddard, John. *Kayaks Down the Nile*. Brigham Young University Press.

Sutherland, Audrey. *Paddling My Own Canoe*. University of Hawaii Press.

Periodicals

Canoe Magazine
Canoe America Associates
P.O. Box 3146
Kirkland, Washington 98083
(206) 827-6363

Mainly covers hardshell boats; very seldom features inflatables—kayaks or otherwise.

Currents
National Organization for River Sports
P.O. Box 6847
Colorado Springs, Colorado 80904

River conservation news, political issues such as boater access rights, some adventure, and how-to.

River Runner Magazine
P.O. Box 458
Fallbrook, California 92028
(619) 723-8155

Good source of current IK and general whitewater information. Consult the June 1988 issue for IK specifications comparison chart.

Sea Kayaker
1670 Duranleau Street
Vancouver, British Columbia
V6H 3S4 Canada
(604) 263-1471

Paddling techniques, and adventure stories for ocean paddlers.

Camping Techniques

Fletcher, Colin. *The New Complete Walker* and *The Complete Walker III*. Alfred A. Knopf Publishers.

Wood, Robert S. *Pleasure Packing for the 80s*. Ten Speed Press.